Biting the Bullet

A comedy

Frank Vickery

Samuel French — London
New York - Toronto - Hollywood

ISBN 0 573 01920 7

Please see page iv for further copyright information

Printed and bound in Great Britain by
Redwood Books, Trowbridge, Wiltshire

BITING THE BULLET

First produced by the Sherman Theatre Company at The
Sherman Theatre, Cardiff, on 15th May, 1996, with the
following cast:

Beryl	Menna Trussler
Ted	Dudley Owen
Dawn	Christine Pritchard
Angie	Cath Tregenna
Scott	Richard Elfyn

Directed by Phil Clark

CHARACTERS

Beryl, 58
Ted, 55
Dawn, middle-aged
Angie, young
Scott, late 20s

The action of the play takes place in the living-room of a semi-detached house

Time: April to early October. The present

SYNOPSIS OF SCENES

ACT I

SCENE 1   Early evening in April
SCENE 2   Later that night
SCENE 3   A month later
SCENE 4   A month later
SCENE 5   A week later

ACT II

SCENE 1   A month later
SCENE 2   The next day
SCENE 3   A month later
SCENE 4   A few days later
SCENE 5   The following week

Other plays by Frank Vickery
published by Samuel French Ltd

Full length:
All's Fair
Breaking the String
Easy Terms
Erogenous Zones
Family Planning
A Kiss on the Bottom
Loose Ends
Love Forty
A Night on the Tiles
One O'Clock from the House
Roots and Wings
Spanish Lies
Trivial Pursuits

One act:
After I'm Gone
Green Favours
A Night Out
Split Ends

ACT I

The living-room of a large semi-detached house. An early evening in April

A door L leads to the hallway and the front door, a door R leads to the kitchen. Along the back are four glass panels, two of which are french windows that open out on to a small patio and garden. There are practical curtains which can cover the entire glass area. There are two settees with cushions. One faces almost front R and another at an angle L. There is a low coffee table placed somewhere in between, on which are some keys and a wallet. There is also a drinks cabinet against the wall UR, a bureau on the wall DL of the kitchen door, a dining chair L of the french windows, and another chair nearby. A couple of small table lamps sit on occasional tables

When the CURTAIN rises, Beryl is pacing up and down the room. She is wearing a very frilly "Laura Ashley-type" dress, which is obviously quite expensive, but nevertheless doesn't suit her. Her coat is over the back of the settee

After some time, she opens the french windows and peers down the garden. She is anxiously waiting for someone. She comes back inside the house. She looks at her watch

Dawn suddenly appears at the french windows carrying a small make-up bag

Dawn Sorry.
Beryl I thought you weren't coming.
Dawn I said I would, didn't I?
Beryl Time's getting on. I thought perhaps something had cropped up.
Dawn I had to wash the tea dishes first. I could have left them but they'd only be there waiting for me when I got back. Dennis would never think of doing them for me. He's stretched out on the settee and he won't move now until it's time to go to bed. Honestly, he's too lazy to get out of his own way. I asked him earlier to go and see if it was raining. "No," he said. "Call the dog in and see if he's wet." (*She puts the make-up bag down on the arm of the settee*)
Beryl No wonder he's put on all that weight.

Dawn gets a dining chair from L *of french windows and places it front* L *of the settee*

Dawn I've told him, "You're turning into a real couch tomato".
Beryl I think it's potato.
Dawn I wouldn't be surprised, he eats enough of them. Now then. Sit here. Let's get you sorted. (*She reaches for her make-up bag*) I've brought in a few bits and pieces of my own.
Beryl (*sitting on the dining chair*) Just as well because I haven't anything myself.
Dawn What? Not even a lipstick?
Beryl I don't wear make-up... I've told you.
Dawn Well ... we're just going to have to do the best we can with this lot then, aren't we? (*During the following, she applies some make-up to Beryl's face*)
Beryl Nothing too heavy. I don't want to look like a painted doll.
Dawn Don't you trust me?
Beryl I don't know why I let you talk me into it in the first place.
Dawn Say the truth, you quite fancied tarting yourself up.
Beryl To be honest, I'm sorry I said I'd go now.
Dawn Too late for cold feet ... not having had your hair done specially *and* bought a nice new frock.
Beryl It's all right, is it? The dress?
Dawn It's lovely, Ber'.
Beryl The trouble with *me* is, I haven't been out for so long——
Dawn It's a real effort for you.
Beryl Yes.
Dawn I just said the same to Dennis. "If you don't start separating yourself from that piece of furniture," I said, "people are going to start talking".
Beryl (*after a pause*) What do you think they'll say?
Dawn It was a joke, Beryl.
Beryl Sorry.
Dawn Don't apologise—Dennis didn't get it either. I think that's enough, don't you?

Beryl gets up and checks herself in the mirror, which is in the fourth wall

Beryl (*quite pleased*) I don't look too bad, do I?
Dawn You look very nice... Ted's not going to know you when he sees you.
Beryl I hope he will... I'm only doing it for him.
Dawn I wouldn't be surprised if we've *both* been wasting our time then, because men never notice anything after the first five years... Mind you, Dennis stopped after the first five months. I could walk back in the house

now naked and he wouldn't even take his eyes off the television. I'm telling you, making yourself look nice for your husband is a complete waste of time.

Beryl So why do you do it?

Dawn I don't any more. I do it for *me* now ... and anyone else who cares to look.

Beryl Ted is bound to notice ... don't you think?

Dawn I wouldn't put money on it. Where is he, anyway?

Beryl Upstairs.

Dawn Well, I've got to go. Let me know how you get on. And don't forget ... enjoy yourself.

Beryl I think I've forgotten how.

Dawn (*replacing the chair* L *of windows*) Get a couple of drinks down you. Have one now, that'll get you going.

Beryl (*crossing* R *to the drinks cabinet*) Will you have one with me?

Dawn Well, I shouldn't really... What have you got?

Beryl Whatever you want ... you know Ted and his drinks cabinet.

Dawn (*sitting on the* L *settee*) I'll have a quick vodka and tonic then.

Beryl pours drinks

Not too strong though... Dennis has got a bad back and drink goes straight to my loins.

Beryl That's a funny place for it to go.

Dawn Three and I'm anybody's.

Beryl I don't know what to have myself.

Dawn You're having the same as me.

Beryl I don't really like alcohol.

Dawn I'm not drinking on my own.

Beryl Well ... perhaps just a small one then.

Dawn You'll probably find it'll relax you ... and you'll need relaxing if you're going to meet all of Ted's work mates. D'you know, I'm amazed this is the first "do" you've been too, and how many years have you been married?

Beryl Thirty-two. (*She hands Dawn her drink*) And it isn't the first.

Dawn Thanks.

Beryl (*sitting on the* R *settee*) I went to one when I was in my thirties. I didn't enjoy it. When we got home we had this huge row and we didn't speak to each other for three weeks. I vowed I'd never go again.

Dawn So what changed your mind this time?

Beryl I don't know.

Dawn What did Ted say when you told him you were coming?

Beryl He said I could please myself.

Dawn He didn't exactly make you feel wanted then?

Beryl I don't think he meant anything by it ... he goes out so often on his own to his meetings and his choir and that, he's probably going to find it strange having *me* in tow.

Dawn And you? How will *you* feel?

Beryl I don't know...

Dawn Thirty-two years married and you're acting like you're going out with him for the first time.

Beryl I know ... but it is the first time in a *long* time. (*She pauses*) It's silly, isn't it?

Dawn No, it's not ... perhaps you'll have a wonderful time and he'll fall in love with you all over again.

Beryl Do you think so?

Dawn It happens.

Beryl likes the idea. She finishes her drink in one

That's my girl ... you go for it.

Ted (*off*) Beryl?

Dawn I'm off. (*She finishes off her drink and heads for the french windows*)

Beryl Thanks for coming in.

Dawn Any time, Ber'. (*She turns to face her*) You look smashin'. Let me know if Ted notices the make-up. (*She rushes off through the french windows, then rushes immediately back to give Beryl her empty glass. She turns to leave*)

Beryl Dawn?

Dawn stops and turns

You're sure I look all right?

Dawn You'll knock 'em dead, Beryl.

Dawn winks and goes

Beryl returns the glasses to the cabinet

Ted comes in from upstairs. He is all dressed and ready to leave. He tosses his coat over the back of the settee as he makes his way to the mirror

Ted *I'm* all ready. I hope *you're* not going to keep the taxi waiting.

Beryl No, I'm ready too.

Ted (*checking himself*) You haven't changed your mind then?

Beryl About what?

Ted The dinner-dance. Still determined to go through with it?

Beryl Determined? You make it sound like I'm coming out of spite. (*She looks at him*)

He looks at her. There is a pause

Ted I still can't work it out. You hate these kind of do's.
Beryl Would you rather I didn't go?
Ted No, no ... you do what you like.
Beryl But you'd prefer it if I stayed home.
Ted You're putting words in my mouth.
Beryl I'm not ... I'm asking you to open wide, that's all.
Ted What?
Beryl To check they're not already there.
Ted (*crossing downstage from the mirror to the coffee table, collecting keys, wallet, etc.*) Look, it doesn't bother me if you come one way or the other, I've told you. (*He puts on the overcoat*)
Beryl That's OK then. (*She pauses*) Do I look all right?
Ted (*without looking up at her*) You look fine.
Beryl How can you tell with your back to me?

He deliberately turns to look at her

Ted What have you done to your face?
Beryl It's just a little make-up. Do you like it?
Ted It doesn't suit you.
Beryl (*crossing to the mirror*) Would you rather I took it off?
Ted It's up to you.
Beryl (*after a pause*) About my dress.
Ted What about it?
Beryl What do you think of it?
Ted (*looking at it*) Too fussy.
Beryl It's Laura Ashley's.
Ted (*going to the drinks cabinet*) You've got a wardrobe full of clothes. What do you want to borrow a dress from her for? (*He spots the empty glasses*) Have you been drinking?
Beryl Just the one.
Ted Two dirty glasses?
Beryl Dawn had one with me ... although it's truer to say I had one with her.
Ted What did she want?
Beryl She didn't want anything. I asked her in to do me a favour. (*She pauses*) I wanted her to tell me that I looked nice. I wanted her to say, "That's a pretty dress, Beryl".
Ted And did she?
Beryl More or less.

Ted And still you needed a second opinion.

Beryl Yes... I wonder what that means? (*She knows*) You could have said something nice about my face. I'd like to think you don't realize how much you hurt me.

Ted (*standing in front of the R settee*) Now for God's sake, Beryl, let's not start that all over again. We're going for a night out, don't spoil it even before the taxi gets here.

Beryl (*crossing to him*) Will you do something for me?

Ted What?

Beryl Will you tell me that you'd really like me to come tonight?

Ted (*impatiently*) I'd really like you to come.

Beryl Will you say it like you mean it?

There is a pause. Suddenly, the taxi horn is heard off

Ted There's the taxi.

Ted leaves

Beryl is left standing in the middle of the room waiting for her answer

After some time, Ted appears in the doorway

The taxi's waiting. (*He pauses*) Are you coming or not?

After a pause, Beryl turns and picks up her coat from the settee. She slowly walks over to Ted, but stops a yard or so from him. She pauses before throwing her coat at him

Ted turns and leaves

Beryl remains there—her shoulders begin to bob as she quietly breaks down

Music plays and the Lights fade

SCENE 2

The same. Later that night

Music fades. The only light to come up is a small table lamp. In the scene change the coat has been picked up from the floor and placed neatly on the back of the chair

Beryl is sitting on the R *settee, still in her Laura Ashley dress. It is twelve thirty a.m., or so. Someone is heard off*

It is Ted coming home from the dinner. He has had a drink but is far from drunk. He comes into the living-room and switches on the lights. He is surprised to see Beryl, who is waiting for him

Ted I thought you'd be in bed.

Beryl You mean you hoped I'd be.

Ted (*checking his watch*) It's half-past twelve. What are you doing up?

Beryl You enjoyed yourself.

Ted Yes.

Beryl It wasn't a question.

Ted It was a good night... You should have come.

Beryl I did.

Ted (*after a pause*) What?

Beryl After you left I pulled myself together, told myself how silly I was... What does it matter if he can't say those things to you, I said. He's never said them before, why is it important he should say them now? (*She pauses*) I phoned a taxi and followed on.

Ted You couldn't have come to the dinner ... someone would have seen you... *I* would have seen you. (*He begins to take off his jacket and loosens his tie*)

Beryl You didn't ... but I saw *you*. If only you knew how hard it was for me to turn up at that place on my own. It was very noisy and too many coloured lights ... somehow I imagined everyone to be waltzing or doing the foxtrot. The last thing I expected was some kind of disco. (*She pauses*) I was just about to ask someone if they knew where you were sitting when I spotted you up on the dance floor. I had no idea you could dance like that ... in fact I thought you didn't like dancing at all.

Ted It was only a bit of fun. I'd never have done it if I hadn't had a couple of drinks first. (*He sits on the arm of the* R *settee*)

Beryl I wish you could have seen yourself ... you looked as though you were showing off...

Ted It's called enjoying yourself. You haven't done it for so long you've forgotten what it looks like.

Beryl I was fascinated... I couldn't take my eyes off you. Suddenly I realized I'm married to the oldest swinger in town.

Ted There's nothing wrong in having a good time.

Beryl You were sweating and breathing so hard I thought you were going to have a heart attack.

Ted (*standing up*) Healthy exercise, that's how *I* look at it. How long did you stand there watching?

Beryl Long enough. It took a minute to realize what was going on.

Ted What do you mean?

Beryl For a while I couldn't see it ... then it hit me like a ton of bricks...
Everyone on the floor continually changed partners ... everyone except
you, that is.

Ted If you've got something to say I'd rather you come out with it. (*He pours
himself a drink from the cabinet*)

Beryl Would you? (*She thinks about it*) Yes, I think you would. Well, I'm
not going to ... that would make it easy for you and I'm not going to do that
... but I would like to know who she is.

Ted Who?

Beryl The woman you danced with for most of the evening.

Ted (*crossing up stage between the settees*) It's not what you think.

Beryl Tell me.

Ted Susanne. Her name is Susanne. She works in accounts. She's just a bit
of a character, that's all. (*He sits on the settee* L)

Beryl Like you, you mean.

Ted Me?

Beryl Every time you whispered something in her ear she laughed hysterically *and* vice versa... I can't remember when you made *me* laugh last.
Have you got anything you want to say to me, Ted?

Ted She's a married woman.

Beryl Where was her husband?

He doesn't answer

  Was *he* there tonight?

Ted He's a rigger ... he works on the rigs. He's only home every sixteen
weeks.

Beryl How long has it been going on?

Ted There's nothing going on.

Beryl You could at least feign *some* insistence.

Ted (*insisting*) There is nothing going on!

Beryl That's more like it.

Ted So you believe me?

Beryl No, not really.

Ted Whether you believe me or not, there's nothing going on.

Beryl Do I detect a disappointed tone hidden away in there somewhere?

Ted I'd be lying if I said I didn't like her.

Beryl So you wish there *was* something going on between you.

Ted (*standing up and moving downstage*) You can deny it as much as you
like, you're putting words in my mouth. (*He pauses*) We see each other in
the canteen. I make her laugh. She's half my age ... what could she possibly
see in me.

Beryl I've asked myself that question all night.

Ted You do believe me then?

Beryl I want to ... but that doesn't make it true.

Ted The truth is ... no, never mind.

Beryl No, tell me.

Ted (*moving downstage of the* L *settee*) It's late. Let's go to bed.

Beryl (*moving to him and physically cutting him off*) Tell me what the truth is.

Ted (*after a pause*) I saw a photograph of me the other day... It was taken at one of the Christmas parties thirty odd years ago. I looked at it and I didn't feel any different. I feel the same now as I did all those years ago. Inside I'm still twenty... Outside I'm fifty-five... That's what the truth is.

Beryl It comes to us all, Ted.

Ted I can't give in.

Beryl You're not going to go hip on me, are you? Please don't tell me you intend collecting your pension at the Post Office wearing trainers, jeans and a rug on your head.

Ted What's wrong with a toupee?

Beryl You don't know?

Ted Colin Baker from marketing's got one and it's knocked ten years off him.

Beryl And put five on everyone else by giving them laugh lines.

Ted You're missing my point.

Beryl No, I'm not. I can see exactly where you're coming from. You're vain, Ted.

Ted No.

Beryl I suppose it would be easier for both of us if you'd always been, but you haven't ... it's come with age. It all seems so incredibly sad, don't you think? Well, no, of course you don't.

Ted (*making to leave*) I'm going to bed.

Beryl She doesn't want you, you know that, don't you? It's not about her though, is it? I can't tell you what to do, Ted. I can't even nudge you in the right direction because it would be towards me, and I'm biased.

Ted I don't want to hurt you.

Beryl But somehow I think you're going to anyway.

Ted There's nothing here for me any more.

Beryl *I'm* here for you.

Ted I think we'll both be better off in the long run.

Beryl (*raising her voice*) Don't you dare speak for me.

Ted Admit there's nothing here for you either.

Beryl If you're not going to be here, no, there isn't. This house isn't you or me. It's both of us.

Ted Why are you painting a rosy picture? Things haven't been good for a long time.

Beryl News to me.
Ted Oh, come on.
Beryl So last Friday night in bed was a figment of my imagination?

They stop and stare at each other. Then he looks away

Ted I can't talk about this now.
Beryl You were wonderful ... the best you've been.

He looks at her again

Ted If you only knew. (*He pauses*) I'm sorry.
Beryl What for?
Ted That wasn't me.
Beryl Don't be ridiculous.
Ted Or you, then... For me it wasn't you. (*He stares at her for a moment*) I couldn't help myself. (*He raises his voice*) Don't tell me during the thirty odd years with me you haven't thought of anyone else.
Beryl No, never!
Ted (*incredulously*) Are you saying you've never once looked up at me and saw Clint Eastwood look back down.
Beryl (*after a pause*) Now I realize this might be one hell of a boost to your ego, Ted, but the answer to that is "No", too.
Ted (*moving away* L) It doesn't mean anything. It's just a harmless fantasy, that's all.
Beryl If it's Clint Eastwood, film star, possibly. If it's Susanne from accounts, it's another story.
Ted The principle's the same. And anyway, I don't remember saying who it was.
Beryl So I'm wrong then, it wasn't her.
Ted No.
Beryl Then who was it?
Ted I don't want to tell you.
Beryl Look, Ted, I have a right to know who you pretended I was last Friday.
Ted And I have a right to my privacy.
Beryl Not when you're mentally commiting adultery, and that's what you were doing, make no mistake.
Ted Well, if I was, I'm sure half the men in the country are as guilty as me.
Beryl You can't justify what you've been doing by telling me fifty per cent of the male population do the same.
Ted But they do.
Beryl How do you know?
Ted Because I do.

Beryl How?
Ted Well, men talk.
Beryl About their sex life?
Ted Only to other men.
Beryl What do they say?
Ted I don't know … things.
Beryl Like what?
Ted Like … things.
Beryl Like who they pretended their wife was last night?
Ted (*moving towards the door*) I'm going to bed.
Beryl Is it the men at work?
Ted Leave it there, will you?
Beryl Friends in the choir? Who?
Ted I can't cope with this. Just forget it.
Beryl Oh, that I could. You've got no idea what you've done, have you? I
  won't be able to face any of your friends any more, in case they know
  what's been going on in our bedroom.
Ted Why are you worrying about what people know or don't know? We've
  got much bigger trouble than that.

She pauses and looks at him. She knows he's talking about the marriage

Beryl You can't be serious about leaving, you've got nowhere to go.
Ted It's time, Beryl. It's not fair to either of us if I stay. (*He pauses*) I'll leave
  in the morning.
Beryl Will you go to *her*?
Ted She's a *friend*.
Beryl You haven't answered me.
Ted I'll sleep in the spare room tonight.
Beryl I thought *I* was your friend.
Ted You're not going to change my mind.
Beryl (*after a pause*) What's going to happen to me?
Ted Don't. I feel guilty enough as it is.
Beryl I'm fifty-eight, what's out there for *me*?

He doesn't answer

  Come to bed. We can talk about it more in the morning.
Ted I should have gone years ago.
Beryl Why didn't you?
Ted (*shrugging his shoulders*) I didn't have the guts, I suppose.
Beryl But you do now?
Ted It's now or never.

Beryl Desperation point. Not the best time to do it.

Ted Since when have *you* been the expert?

Beryl Since now ... since I've had to be.

Ted It's over, Beryl. We know it's dead. It's about time we both got round to burying it. (*Almost at the door*)

Beryl (*calling after him*) Ted? I'd like the truth. (*She pauses*) Who did you pretend I was last Friday? (*She waits for an answer*)

He looks away then looks back at her. She realizes he isn't going to give her the answer

Eventually Ted leaves

She stands rooted to the spot as she quietly breaks down

Music plays and the Lights fade

SCENE 3

The same. Late morning, a month later

Music fades and the Lights come up

There is an empty bottle of something tucked underneath one of the scatter cushions. The curtains to the french windows are closed but a chink of daylight is finding its way through. A small table lamp is on but it is only offering minimal light

Beryl is slumped on the L settee

Suddenly, the front door slams. Beryl stirs but doesn't wake

Angie (*off*) Mum? Mum, are you there?

Angie comes into the living-room and sees Beryl on the chair

Mum? What's the matter, are you ill? I've been ringing you since yesterday. I didn't know what to expect when Dawn got in touch.

Beryl (*groggy*) Dawn? (*She moves to a slightly upright position*)

Angie (*going to open the curtains*) She's been knocking and couldn't get an answer. She thought you might have died or something.

Beryl My God, I think I have.

Angie What's going on?
Beryl What day is it?
Angie Friday. How long have you been like this?
Beryl I don't know... Is it still May?

Angie opens the curtains. The room fills with light

Angie I'm going to ring the doctor.
Beryl No, don't do that. I'm not ill.
Angie What are you, then?
Beryl (*retrieving the empty bottle from behind the cushion*) Drunk.
Angie You don't drink.
Beryl (*placing the bottle on the floor*) I do now.
Angie (*seeing the bottle*) Did *you* empty that?
Beryl Yes, but don't worry, it's taken me days.
Angie (*after a pause*) It's Dad, isn't it?
Beryl Well, it's not the man who comes to read the meter.
Angie (*taking the empty bottle and putting it in the drinks cabinet*) It's been a month now, Mum... He's not coming back.
Beryl Don't say that... The hope that he's going to walk through that door is the only thing that's keeping me going.
Angie (*sitting on the settee*) You were doing OK. What happened?

Beryl doesn't answer

Have you heard from him?
Beryl A couple of days ago.
Angie He came here?
Beryl He rang first. He said he wanted to see me. I'm not going to take him back straight away, I thought ... make him grovel a bit first, you know ... teach him a lesson. (*She tries not to get upset, then she tries to laugh*) He didn't want to come back at all. He just wanted to make arrangements to pick up his drinks cabinet. Can you believe that?

Dawn appears outside the french windows. She taps on the glass

Angie gets up and lets her in

Dawn Everything all right, is it?
Angie Yeah ... she's just a bit fragile, that's all.
Dawn Oh, good. I was ever so worried, Beryl. I thought you might have topped yourself or something. I know how down you've been the last couple of weeks.

Angie Shall I put the kettle on?

Dawn Good idea. One sugar if it's a cup, two if it's a mug. Not too strong, with just a smattering of milk.

Angie Mum?

Dawn As it comes.

Angie (*quietly in Dawn's ear*) Have a chat to her. Try and buck her up, she's really down at the moment.

Angie goes off into the kitchen

Dawn stands to the left of the settee and looks over at Beryl

Dawn (*not quite sure what to say*) Oh dear ... you really do look a mess this morning, don't you?

Beryl holds her head in her hands

I bet you could do with a nice hot bath.

Beryl Do you think I should give it to him?

Dawn What?

Beryl Ted wants the cabinet. Should I let him have it?

Dawn I don't know.

Angie (*off*) Biscuit?

Dawn (*calling back*) Ooh, yes please.

Angie (*off*) Mum?

Beryl (*calling to her*) There's none there.

Dawn (*disappointed*) Oh.

Beryl She'll be lucky to find a tea-bag.

Dawn (*joining her on the settee*) You haven't done any shopping, have you?

Beryl I haven't been in the mood.

Dawn Well, you write a little list and I'll get it all for you this afternoon.

Beryl I don't even know when I went out last.

Dawn Better still, I'll take you with me.

Beryl No.

Dawn You'll do yourself no good staying indoors. The sooner you get out, the sooner you'll stop the tongues wagging.

Beryl What tongues? Are people talking?

Dawn Well, it's only natural. Not that *I've* said anything. I'm the soul of discretion, you know that.

Beryl What are they saying?

Dawn I try not to listen, really.

Beryl Tell me.

Dawn I refused to comment when they asked me.

Beryl I want to know.
Dawn "Look", I said, "she's a friend of mine, it's difficult for me".
Beryl (*raising her voice*) Tell me what they're saying!
Dawn They said you caught him in bed with another woman.
Beryl That's not true.
Dawn I said it wasn't.
Beryl Did you?
Dawn Well, I said I'd find out.
Beryl Well, it's not.
Dawn I thought so.
Beryl And anyway, he's coming back.
Dawn Is he?
Beryl Yes.
Dawn Then why has he asked for his cabinet?
Beryl That was just an excuse ... you know, to see me.
Dawn (*after eyeing Beryl up*) Right. (*She does not believe this for a minute*)

Angie comes in from the kitchen

Angie It won't be long. (*To Dawn*) How is she doing?

Dawn goes to her. Both are standing just behind the R settee

Dawn I don't like it. She seems all right on the surface but she's going into denial. Could be dangerous later on.
Beryl I *can* hear you, you know.
Dawn I'm just worried about you, that's all. My cousin went through the same sort of thing when her husband committed adultery.
Beryl (*insisting*) Ted has not committed adultery!
Dawn (*to Angie*) See what I mean? We're going to have to keep an eye on her. It's exactly the same behaviour pattern as my cousin.
Angie And what happened to her?
Dawn She hung herself on the landing.
Beryl I'm not going to do anything silly like that.
Dawn My cousin said the same words exactly.
Beryl I'm not!
Dawn I think the kettle's boiling. You keep an eye on her and I'll do the rest.

Dawn goes out into the kitchen

Angie (*after a pause*) Are you going to be all right, Mum?
Beryl She's a nice girl, Angie, I like her, but she doesn't know what the hell she's talking about.

Angie Listen, about Dad. (*She sits on the* R *settee*) I don't understand why you're not glad to see the back of him. He treated you awfully.

Beryl That was just his way... He's always been the same, you know that. (*She pauses*) Do you know what he said when he first asked me out?

Angie shakes her head

Well, it's more *how* he said it, really. He walked across the dance floor straight to where I was sitting, stood in front of me and said, "I'm going out tomorrow night and I want you there by half-past seven".

Angie Cheeky sod. Did you go?

Beryl No.

Angie Good for you.

Beryl I *would* have, but in his arrogance he didn't tell me where to meet him.

Angie What did you see in him?

Beryl doesn't answer

I saw this coming, you know.

Beryl Yes, it's my fault.

Angie No. (*She goes to her*) No, it's not your fault at all.

Beryl You're only saying that to make me feel better.

Angie (*moving to sit next to Beryl on the* L *settee*) I'm saying it because it's the truth. It's natural you'll blame yourself when you're going through this sort of thing ... but when you come out the other side ... you'll see. You're not the one that's wrong here, Mum.

Beryl I should have gone out with him more.

Angie Maybe, but you didn't push him into anyone's arms.

Beryl (*shouting*) He's not *in* anyone's arms! (*She considers it*) Is he?

Angie struggles to answer, then shrugs her shoulders

What do you know?

Angie Nothing.

Beryl You're keeping something from me. I want to know what it is.

Angie There's nothing.

Beryl Don't lie to me.

Angie I'm not.

Beryl He's with *her*, isn't he?

Angie I've no idea.

Beryl He told me when he came here he was staying in some bed and breakfast place.

Dawn comes in carrying a tray with three mugs on it

Angie Look, he's gone... Just let him get on with his life.
Beryl I know you're only trying to protect me but I want to know where he's living.
Dawn According to the woman in the Post Office, he's with that girl from accounts.

Angie looks at her incredulously

Well, it's best she knows... (*She puts the tray down on the coffee table*) She's never going to get over it if she doesn't face things head on.
Beryl (*upset*) And to think he denied it all the time he was here.
Angie Maybe he's *not* with her.
Dawn Yes, it's possible. You know what rumours are like. Monday he's living with her, Friday she's having his baby.

Beryl cries even more

(*Handing a mug to Angie*) At the end of the day it's best not to take any notice. (*She hands a mug to Beryl*) Drink this... I'm sure it'll make you feel better. (*She sits down on the R settee. She pauses*) It's difficult to know what to say in situations like this, isn't it? (*She remembers something*) Oh. (*She mouths to Angie*) I've hidden all the knives in the cupboard above the extractor fan. (*She smiles*) I thought it best.

Dawn's smile fades as she sees Beryl's stony face

Perhaps I should put them back.
Beryl Yes, I think you should.
Dawn It's just that if you were to——
Beryl What?
Dawn You know... (*She mimes slitting a wrist, then cutting her throat*) Well, I'd never forgive myself.
Beryl (*very firmly*) Can I just make one thing perfectly clear? However depressed I am, or you *think* I am, I've got no intention of doing anything to myself that I might regret later. Now is that understood?

No-one replies

(*Insisting*) Is that understood?
Angie Yes.
Beryl (*firmly*) Dawn?
Dawn Yes. (*She pauses*) Excuse me while I go and turn the gas back on at the mains.

Dawn goes out into the kitchen

A pause

Angie She cares about you. (*She pauses*) You did mean what you said, didn't
you?

Beryl looks up at her

You *wouldn't* try to blow yourself up or anything.
Beryl I'm already finished, Angie... There's nothing left to destroy.
Angie You mustn't talk like that. Don't look at this as the end... It's the
beginning.
Beryl That's the trouble when you build your world around one person. At
least that's something they can't accuse *you* of.
Angie (*smiling as she pretends to be outraged*) I haven't had *that* many.
Beryl Go on ... you've had more fellas than I've had cooked dinners.

Dawn comes in from the kitchen

Dawn (*really excited*) Look what I found on the floor behind the cooker. (*She
holds up a Club biscuit*)
Angie What is it?
Dawn (*standing behind the coffee table*) A Club biscuit. My favourite... But
heaven knows when you ate last, Beryl, so I think *you* should have it.
Beryl I don't want it.
Dawn Are you sure?

Beryl dismisses it with her hand

Angie?
Angie Not for me.

Dawn pauses for a moment, then reluctantly puts it down on the coffee table

Don't *you* want it?
Dawn Well, I didn't like ... you know.
Beryl Eat it, Dawn ... it'll only go in the bin.

Dawn looks from Beryl to Angie, then slowly takes the biscuit and unwraps it

Dawn Well, they *are* my favourites.

A pause

Angie (*standing up*) Well... I've got a client in half an hour. I'm going to have to go in a minute.

Beryl Before you do... (*She pauses*) If you knew your father *was* living with that woman, you would tell me, wouldn't you? (*She looks at her*)

Angie eventually nods

Dawn I don't want to be a thorn in your side...

Both Beryl and Angie look at her

(*Biting into her chocolate biscuit*) Well, I think it's best to be realistic, don't you?

Angie If I hear anything, Mum, I'll let you know. (*She pauses*) You'll be all right now, won't you?

Dawn (*collecting the mugs and putting them on the tray*) She'll be fine. I'm not going to let her out of my sight.

Angie You've got my number, anyway, Dawn.

Dawn Yes. Just one thing. *If* anything untoward was to happen ... who should I phone first, you or the emergency services?

Beryl Angie, don't even answer that.

Angie I'll see you tomorrow then.

Beryl You don't *have* to.

Angie I know that ... but I can if I want to ... right? (*She kisses her mother on the cheek*)

Dawn Ahh, isn't that nice?

Beryl (*to Angie*) I don't know when you kissed me last.

Angie Christmas.

Beryl That's right, when me and your father...

A pause

Angie I'll see you in the morning.

Angie turns and leaves

We hear the front door close

Dawn She's a lovely girl. I don't think I've ever kissed *my* mother... I don't know when I kissed Dennis last. (*She laughs as she joins Beryl on the settee*) That was a joke, Beryl. I kissed him last Thursday.

Beryl I know, I heard you through the bedroom wall.

Dawn Honestly?

Beryl Dennis might be too lazy to get out of his way, Dawn, but he can certainly rustle up enough energy when he wants to.

Dawn You mean you know when we…

Beryl nods. A pause

Do you hear us every month?

Beryl doesn't answer

(*Sipping her tea*) I suppose you miss that side of things too, don't you?

Beryl doesn't answer

Perhaps if I was to have a word with Dennis.

Beryl What?

Dawn It can't be very pleasant for you at this time. Perhaps he can help you out.

Beryl looks at her, almost horrified

I'll get him to pull our headboard away from the wall for you.

Beryl (*almost smiling*) You know, for a minute there … never mind, forget it.

Dawn Is that a smile I see?

Beryl (*slowly the smile disappears*) If he *is* living in that woman's house, it doesn't necessarily mean he's sleeping with her … does it?

Dawn I know it's hard, my love … but you will get over it. (*She moves towards the R door*) Now I'm going to run you a nice hot bath.

Beryl I'm not going out!

Dawn Oh, yes you are. You're coming with me this afternoon and you're going to hold your head up. You're going to let everyone know you don't give a damn that Ted's been putting it around for years.

Beryl Has he?

Dawn According to the woman in the Post Office.

Beryl Oh God.

Dawn But you mustn't let it get the better of you. Just remember, "He who shags last, shags the longest".

Beryl (*after a pause*) What's that supposed to mean?

Dawn I'm not sure… Think about it while I run your water.

Dawn goes out

Beryl is left to ponder

Music plays and the Lights fade

SCENE 4

The same. Mid-afternoon, a month later

Music fades and the Lights come up

Angie is walking Beryl around the room. She is supporting her by holding her arm around her neck. Her other arm is around her waist. Beryl is semi-conscious and is taking some of her own weight. They have both walked from UR *to* DL

Dawn comes in from the kitchen. She is carrying a tray with a mug of hot water, a spoon and a jar of Nescafé on it

Dawn I knew something like this was going to happen. (*She sets the tray down on the coffee table*) I think I know what's tipped her over the edge, too. I've been asking Dennis for a month now to move our bed.
Angie What's your bed got to do with anything?
Dawn It's only a couple of inches, I said, but I may as well be asking for a foot.
Angie That's it, Mum ... keep walking.

Dawn spoons six or seven spoonfuls of coffee into the mug

Dawn If this doesn't do any good, Angie, you're going to *have* to phone the doctor. Perhaps that's not such a bad idea anyway. Between you and me, I think she needs *professional* help now.
Angie I want to try one last thing.
Dawn What's that?
Angie All in good time. Come on, Mum. Come and have a drink.

Angie brings Beryl to sit on the settee. She sits next to her. She takes the mug from Dawn and holds it to her mother's mouth. Beryl sips

Dawn She was all right yesterday. She even said she was going to have her hair done. Do you think her stomach needs pumping?
Angie Not judging by how many tablets are left.
Dawn You reckon she wasn't serious about it, then?
Angie She was serious enough to leave a note.
Dawn (*amazed*) She wrote a suicide note? What did it say?
Angie I don't know, it's not addressed to me.

Dawn (*after a pause*) She wrote it to your father?

Angie nods as she tries to get Beryl to drink a little more

I don't know why she wrote to him. I think it's criminal what he's done to her.

Beryl (*very groggy*) Oh God.

Dawn Good, she's coming round.

Angie Have some more. (*She forces her to have another sip*)

Beryl Where am I?

Dawn You're all right, Beryl... We caught you in the nick of time.

Beryl sort of comes round and looks at each of them in turn. She then seems to realize who they are and where she is. She becomes upset

Beryl Oh God, what have I done.

Angie It's all right, Mum. Everything's going to be all right.

Beryl I'm sorry.

Dawn It could happen to anyone.

Beryl I'm so sorry.

Dawn Try not to think about ... it. I'd be embarrassed too if I tried to kill myself and didn't pull it off.

Beryl (*to Angie*) It's not that I don't love you.

Angie I know.

Beryl But there doesn't seem to be a purpose anymore.

Dawn Chronic depression if ever I saw it.

Angie We're going to get you through this.

Dawn What happened? You were doing so well.

Beryl No I wasn't. I know you all *thought* I was, but all the time I was going under. (*She pauses*) I went to the hairdresser's yesterday——

Angie So you *did* go, then?

Dawn (*pulling pieces of Beryl's hair about*) You shouldn't have wasted your money, Ber'.

Angie You wanted to look nice, yes?

Beryl I was there for twenty minutes before I realized who was under the dryer.

Angie Who was it?

Dawn Never her from accounts?

Beryl She was telling everyone she was having her hair done because she's flying to Cyprus the day after tomorrow.

Dawn What did you do?

Beryl I'm not sure. I know I made a scene. One minute I was standing in the salon with a head full of rollers, and the next I was back home here in my bathroom.

Angie You can't go on like this, Mum. Harming yourself isn't the answer.

Beryl But I don't know what else is. I'm not even sure where I am any more.

Dawn Oh, *I* know. You're on the floor, my love. You've hit rock bottom, that's what you've done. But you're not to worry, because once you've sunk that low there's only one other way to go, and that's up. Am I right, Angie?

Angie I hope so.

Suddenly, the doorbell rings

Dawn I'll get it.

Dawn goes off to answer it

Angie (*after a pause*) You didn't half give me a fright. You promised you'd never try that sort of thing.

Beryl I know ... but something came over me.

Angie (*after a pause*) How are you feeling now?

Beryl (*after a pause*) Very silly ... and I've got a thumping headache.

Angie (*playfully*) Serve you right. (*She pauses*) I've had an idea. I thought of it this morning.

Beryl What is it?

Dawn re-appears just inside the living-room door. She pauses

(*To Dawn*) What is it?

Dawn Um...

Angie What's wrong?

Beryl Who was at the door?

Dawn (*after a pause*) It's Ted.

Beryl (*panicking*) Don't let him in. Don't let him see me like this.

Dawn He wants to talk to you, Beryl.

Beryl Please.

Angie It'll be all right, Mum.

Beryl No ... I'm not ready.

Angie OK. Dawn, take her somewhere.

Dawn Like?

Angie I don't know. The garden. Walk her round the garden. Stay out there till he's gone.

Dawn How will I know when that is?

Angie (*almost shouting*) I'll call you.

Beryl and Dawn disappear through the french windows and out of sight

Angie sighs. She positions herself in the room ready to face her father

   Eventually Ted comes in

Ted I've come to see your mother. (*He pauses*) Does she know I'm here? I only want to know if she's all right.
Angie Since when do *you* care?
Ted Let me see her, I haven't got all day.
Angie Of course you haven't. Got to rush back to pack, haven't you?
Ted What?
Angie Look, why don't you tell me what you want, then bugger off to Cyprus.
Ted Cyprus?
Angie And do us a favour and don't send a card.
Ted You think I'd do something like that?
Angie Let's be honest, you've done worse. I think you'd better go.
Ted Not till I've seen your mother.
Angie What for? (*She thinks she knows the reason*) Don't tell me, you've got a joint passport and you need it, right? Well, I'll burn it before you get your hands on it.
Ted I don't need a passport.
Angie Got your own, I suppose.
Ted I'm not going abroad.
Angie Don't lie... That woman said——
Ted *Susanne* is going to Cyprus in the morning... So is Martin. And before you ask who Martin is, he's her husband.

There is a pause

Angie OK, so we got it wrong. It doesn't change anything.
Ted I told your mother when I left there was nothing going on between me and Susanne. It was true then and it's true now. (*He pauses*) Look, there was a bit of a to-do in the hairdresser's yesterday. I just wanted to know if she's all right.
Angie Why would you want to know that?
Ted I do think about her.
Angie Well, isn't that kind.
Ted It's been thirty-two years, you can't just rub it out.
Angie (*standing in front of the* R *settee*) You're having a pretty good try. (*She pauses*) She had a brainstorm yesterday. What happened in the hairdresser's was a sort of blow out. She rang me when she got home and told me she felt better for it. Somehow everything came gushing out like

pus from a nasty boil. But it's over now. It's all cleaned up and beginning to heal. She told me she feels better than she has for months.

Ted You're not going to let me see her, are you?

Angie I don't think it's a good idea. She's looking great these days and the last thing either of us want is for you to start having regrets.

Ted She really is all right?

Angie Cloud nine.

Ted So now would be as good a time as any.

Angie For what?

Ted (*finding it difficult to continue*) I need to talk to her.

Angie You've got to get past *me* first.

Ted I want a divorce. (*He pauses*) It's been a couple of months now and I want to set the wheels in motion.

Angie So much for calling in to see how she was.

Ted I wasn't going to ask her for it today—but when you said how good she was——

Angie What was that you were saying about rubbing her out?

Ted It's time to move on.

Angie She's knocking sixty—where is *she* going to move on to?

Dawn and Beryl appear at the french windows

Beryl Where is he?

Dawn No, Beryl … wait.

Suddenly, they are both standing inside the house. Beryl is still needing a little physical support. Beryl and Ted look at each other

Ted Is she drunk?

Angie We've been celebrating.

Beryl I've got one thing to say to you, Ted Stevens. (*She pauses*) If you've come to borrow a suitcase, you can forget it.

Ted Suitcase? No, Beryl … you've got it wrong.

Angie We've all been at the champagne. It's a private party, so I think you'd better leave.

Beryl Yes, go on … bugger off. (*She pauses before shouting*) I said bugger off!

Ted looks at her, then at Angie, before leaving the room

I've got to sit down.

Beryl and Dawn sit on the L *settee. A pause*

Well, come on, tell me what he wanted.

Angie shrugs and shakes her head

Dawn Maybe it was a last look at you, in case the plane went down.
Beryl (*after a pause*) I wish *I* was going on holiday.
Angie Do you? Good. That's exactly what I've got planned.
Beryl Don't be silly, I can't go away. Tell me what your father wanted.
Angie You need a change of scenery.
Dawn That's right, to get away from it all.
Beryl Are you serious?
Angie (*crouching by the* L *settee*) Let's grab a week away. I could do with it myself… And then you can come back to a fresh start.
Beryl It's a nice idea, but my problems will still be here waiting for me.
Dawn But you'll be in a better frame of mind to tackle them.
Beryl (*to Dawn*) Oh, I don't know. (*To Angie*) And you still haven't answered me.
Dawn I wish someone would offer to take me away for a week.
Angie Wouldn't Dennis?
Dawn The only time he took me anywhere was to Merthyr Tydfil… And then it was to help him bump-start his car.
Angie Come with us if you like.
Dawn What?
Beryl You could—you haven't got any commitments. (*To Angie*) About your father——
Dawn No, I couldn't dream of it. Where are you thinking of going?
Angie Anywhere you like. Benidorm, Italy, the Costa del Sol.
Beryl Anywhere but Cyprus, right?
Angie What do you say?
Dawn Oh, I don't know.
Beryl (*insisting*) Angie—tell me about your father.
Angie In a minute.
Dawn It's very tempting.
Angie What's it to be, then?
Dawn Just for the week, you said?

Angie nods

Angie She'll go if *you* will.
Dawn Ohhh, you've gone and put me right on the spot now, haven't you?
Angie It'll be great … all girls together.
Dawn Seems too good an opportunity to miss.
Angie So is it settled?
Dawn (*after a pause*) Yes, all right then.
Angie I'll go and book us something this afternoon.

Dawn What will my Dennis say?
Angie Don't tell him. Send him a card when you get there. (*She laughs*)

Dawn laughs hysterically, then stops abruptly

Dawn That's not a bad idea, actually.
Beryl Wait a minute, wait a minute, this is all wrong.
Dawn What is?
Beryl Everything's happening too quickly.
Angie What's the matter with that?
Dawn No, I think I agree.
Angie You're not going to change your mind?
Dawn I don't know.
Angie Oh, great.
Beryl Maybe we should take time to think it through ... thoroughly.
Dawn Yes.
Angie Why? It's a good idea, isn't it?
Beryl But it all seems to have happened so fast.
Angie Some things don't stand thinking about. Look, what's the problem?
Dawn Well, mine's next door, lying on the settee.
Beryl One minute I'm being walked round the room because I tried to commit suicide and the next I'm flying off to the sun somewhere.
Angie Nothing wrong in that. It's called living, Mum. What do you say, Dawn?
Dawn Oh, I don't know.
Beryl I think a decision like this deserves careful consideration.
Dawn So do I.
Beryl So let's all take five minutes just to catch our breath.
Dawn Yes.
Angie Fine, but first let's vote on it. All in favour of buggering off, say "Ay".

All three raise their hands and say "ay" simultaneously. Then they all look at each other and fall about laughing

Black-out. Music

SCENE 5

Late afternoon, a week later

Music fades and the Lights come up. The curtains to the french windows are closed, although it is pretty obvious it is daylight outside. After a moment, voices are heard off. Then the front door slams

Beryl comes into the room, followed by Angie who is carrying a case,
rucksack and a duty-free bag. She puts it down immediately

Beryl I'll put the kettle on. (*She goes to the kitchen*) I've never been so glad
to see my own four walls.
Angie Come on, it wasn't *that* bad.
Beryl You speak for yourself.

Beryl goes into the kitchen

Angie So the whole thing was a complete waste of time, then?

Angie opens the curtains and daylight spills in

Beryl (*off*) I wouldn't go so far as to say that.
Angie It was nice to hear you laugh again, and you did, you know ... once
or twice.
Beryl (*off*) Oh, I'm not sorry I went.
Angie Well, that's *something* at least.
Beryl (*off*) It was good to spend some time together.
Angie *I* thought so. Listen. Don't make tea for me, I'm not staying.

Beryl comes in from the kitchen

Beryl In a funny kind of way I'm glad Dawn didn't come. (*She plumps up
cushions on the* L *settee*)

Angie goes to get the mail from the hall

That sounds awful, I know, but what I mean is, it gave us the chance to get
to know each other a bit more.
Angie (*off*) We knew each other pretty well before we went.
Beryl No, you know what I mean. You *think* you know everything about
your children, and then you learn something new.

Angie comes back into the room

Angie Like what for instance? I'm not staying, did you hear? (*She puts the
mail down on the coffee table*)
Beryl Well, like, I had no idea you had a fetish for feet until you got drunk
one night and told me.
Angie Dear God, did I tell you that?

Beryl smiles and nods

Did it shock you?

Beryl Not at the time… I didn't know what a "fetish" meant until I looked it up.

Angie Were you embarrassed?

Beryl No. As soon as I understood the word I realized I had one myself for necks.

Angie Really?

Beryl (*plumping up the cushions on the* R *settee*) I've always had a strange fascination for the nape of the neck… Well, your father's, there's never been anyone else's.

Angie (*sorting out the duty-free bag*) No-one at all?

Beryl No. (*She pauses*) Whenever I used to see it, which wasn't often, I always had this strange, well, urge I suppose you'd call it, to kiss it. (*She is caught in the memory of it for a second, then quickly comes out of it and smiles rather coyly at Angie*) Now I'm embarrassed.

Angie There's no need. We should be able to tell each other everything. (*She pauses*) A couple of times when we were away I thought you wanted to say something to me.

Beryl No. A few times I thought you wanted to say something to *me*.

Angie Like what?

Beryl (*sorting out the mail then placing it on top of the bureau*) I don't know… I often felt you were leading the conversation but I had no idea where.

Angie No, I don't think so.

Beryl It must have been cross wires, then. Or the drink. I've never drank so much in my life.

Angie You didn't get drunk once.

Beryl No, but I never used to drink at all, remember. Now I've even bought fifty pounds worth of the stuff from duty-free.

Angie Who will you share it with?

Beryl I don't know … anyone who knocks my door, I suppose.

Angie Anyone but "Him", right?

Beryl (*after a pause*) We've had thirty-two years together, Angie… Sometimes I hate him for what he's done, but I'd be lying if I told you I didn't love him. They're so close, aren't they, love and hate. I had no idea.

Angie He doesn't deserve you.

Beryl He hasn't got me.

Angie Oh, yes he has. If he turned up now this minute, you'd take him back, wouldn't you?

Beryl Yes. Whatever it was like before … my life's better with him than without him.

Angie It might not always be.

Beryl But it is now … and now is all I've got. He will come back, I know
he will. I feel it.

Angie Look… (*She pauses*) You were right.

Beryl looks at her, she doesn't understand her

I did almost tell you something when we were away. (*She pauses*) Before
we went … when he came here, do you remember?

Beryl nods

He wanted to see you and I wouldn't let him. He wanted to ask you
something. I didn't tell you because I knew it was the last thing you'd want
to hear then.

Beryl (*sitting on the* L *settee*) I've got a feeling it's the last thing I want to hear
now. (*She pauses*) He wants a divorce, doesn't he?

Angie doesn't answer

Doesn't he?

Angie Yes. (*She stands by the* R *settee*) Give it to him.

Beryl I've never refused him anything.

Angie Well, then…

Beryl (*almost in her own world*) Why do I feel he's going to come back?

Angie I'm no psychologist, but I reckon that's all part of the refusing to let
go, don't you?

Beryl (*after a pause*) What's going to happen to me?

Angie Nothing.

Beryl I don't want to be on my own. I don't know how to.

Angie Yes you do. You've been on your own for the past three months.

Beryl And just look at the mess I've made.

Angie I'm not saying it's going to be easy, but you've done the hard bit.
Things will get better now, I promise.

Beryl (*after a pause*) I never saw myself living alone. It frightens me.

Angie Now perhaps, but you'll get to love it. I mean, look at me.

A lawnmower is heard starting up, out in the garden

Beryl I'm not you.

Angie I'll never live with anyone again.

Beryl No, you send them home in the mornings.

Angie Cheeky. (*She pauses*) I know you're still hurting … but this can be
a really exciting time if you want it to be.

Beryl That's the trouble, I don't. I'm too old to be excited. I want comfort now, and company. I need someone to fuss over.

Angie *I* can move back in.

Beryl Oh God, no!

Angie (*laughing*) You can't be *that* desperate then.

Beryl Angie, you're my daughter, and I love you, but a week together is enough. What's that noise?

Angie I can't hear anything.

Beryl Yes, listen.

They do. Beryl walks around the room and eventually ends up at the french windows. She unlocks and opens them. The noise gets slightly louder. She steps just outside and looks down towards the garden

There's someone down there.

Angie Who is it?

Beryl (*stepping back inside*) I don't know. Go and have a look.

Angie Why me?

Beryl You're braver than I am. (*She is almost pushing Angie out of the french windows*) Go on … see what he's up to. Ask him what he's doing in my garden.

Angie walks off towards the garden

Beryl comes back inside and waits, hesitantly. The lawnmower stops. The seconds pass. She eventually decides to have another look. After stretching her neck in several directions, she hurries back inside the house. She positions herself DL

Angie comes in, followed by Scott, who remains just outside the french windows. He is a man in his late twenties. He is wearing an old pair of trainers, jeans that are torn, and a vest which flatters his good physique

What's going on?

Angie It's all right, Mum … it's only Scott.

Beryl Who?

Scott (*stepping just inside the room*) Hi.

Angie Your gardener.

Beryl I haven't got a gardener.

Angie Well, you have now.

Beryl Sorry?

Scott Someone rang and asked to have the lawn cut back and front?

Beryl When was this?

Scott Two … maybe three days ago.

Angie We've only just got back into the country … we've been away for a
   week.
Scott Anywhere nice?
Angie Alcudia.
Scott Nice enough.

*They both enter into a conversation, forgetting for a moment that Beryl is
there*

Angie Have you been there?
Scott Two years ago.
Beryl Excuse me?
Angie It's a drag from the airport, but it's great once you're there.
Scott (*agreeing*) I much prefer the north of the island.
Angie Yes, me too.
Beryl Now, this phone call.
Angie We booked last minute, so we didn't know where we were staying,
   but we did know it was towards the top of the island.
Scott You had a good deal then?
Beryl Hello. Anyone know I'm here?
Angie Oh, a snip… I might even afford to do it again at the end of the summer.
Scott I used to work abroad a lot … but I've stayed home the last couple of
   years.
Angie And where *is* home?
Scott Roath. I've got a flat there… Well, it's not mine, it's my girlfriend's.

Angie immediately turns and steps further into the room

Beryl (*raising her voice*) About my garden.
Angie (*even louder*) Yes, about my mother's garden…
Beryl There's been a mistake obviously.
Scott It happens all the time. I keep telling her, "Get the customer to repeat
   the address". Don't worry, I'll finish up. I'm almost done anyway. There'll
   be no charge, of course.
Angie I'm off. (*To Beryl*) I'll ring you later.
Scott I'm sorry to bother you, but could I use your bathroom? It's thirsty
   work out there and I need to go. I'll take my shoes off, of course.
Beryl Up the stairs, second door on the left.

*He slips off his trainers and steps barefoot inside. Angie is immediately
drawn to his feet*

   Scott hands his shoes to Angie before disappearing off

Angie stares at the shoes in her hand

I'll speak to you later then.

Angie What?

Beryl (*moving to the front of the* R *settee*) Do you think you could stop thinking about his feet for a minute and listen to me?

Angie I wasn't thinking about his feet.

Beryl gives her a disbelieving look

I wasn't.

Beryl Is that how it works these days?

Angie What?

Beryl I remember when a girl waited for the man to make the first move, and if he didn't, she either forgot about him or asked a friend to mediate. Today all that seems to have gone out of the window.

Angie I still don't know what you're talking about.

Beryl I'm talking about you, and how you manoeuvred yourself. If I hadn't seen it with my own eyes I wouldn't have believed it.

Angie I'm not interested in the gardener.

Beryl You were right up until he mentioned the flat and the girlfriend.

Angie I was just making polite conversation, that's all.

Beryl You were making a move. I'm slow, but even I knew you were sowing the seeds for a week away with him ... "at the end of the summer".

Angie I didn't say that for *his* benefit.

Beryl Well, you certainly didn't say it for mine.

Suddenly Dawn appears at the french windows

Dawn (*very excited*) You're back then! (*She comes inside*)

There are hugs all round

Don't tell me, you had a wonderful trip and had the holiday of a lifetime.

Angie You really would have enjoyed it, wouldn't she, Mum?

Beryl It was very mean of Dennis not to let you come.

Dawn I blame myself, really. I should have put my foot down. I coaxed him for hours. I was furious when you left for the airport.

Angie I hope you gave him a piece of your mind.

Dawn I called him an overweight misogynistic pig.

Beryl I didn't know Dennis was a misogynist.

Dawn He doesn't think we should be friends any more.

Beryl You and Dennis?

Dawn No, me and you. He thinks you're a bad influence.

Angie I hope you told him where to go.

Dawn I would have, but we're not speaking. I've had nothing to do with him since I waved you off in the taxi.

Beryl You mean you haven't spoken to him in over a week?

Dawn Or ironed a shirt or even slept with him. I'm still in the spare room. He thought he'd get round me by cutting the grass, but he only got the mower out of the garage and he had to go and lie down for ten minutes. Needless to say, he never went back to it. He phoned someone in the end, (*she laughs*) but as luck would have it, they haven't turned up.

Beryl I'm afraid he's upstairs.

Dawn Who?

Angie The gardener.

Dawn I don't understand.

Angie It's very simple. Your lawnmower man got the wrong address.

Beryl We came home to find him cutting my lawn.

Angie (*handing the shoes to Dawn*) And now he's upstairs having a pee. I really do have to dash. I'll have clients queuing at the door.

Dawn (*handing the shoes to Beryl*) You can't leave now, I've come in to find out all about the holiday.

Angie She'll give you her version. I'm back here in the morning. You can hear the best bits then.

Beryl hands the shoes to Angie

(*To Beryl*) Ring you later. (*Realizing she has the shoes again, she hands them back to Beryl*) Bye.

Angie goes

Dawn What did she mean, "Clients at the door"? You don't have clients in a pub.

Beryl Oh, she's an aromatherapist now... Either that or she's on the game. (*She sits on the L settee*) Anyway, what sort of a week have you had? (*She puts the shoes on the floor*)

Dawn (*joining her on the settee*) I've started night classes. Hairdressing.

Beryl Really? I didn't know you were interested in that sort of thing.

Dawn I wasn't. I just wanted something to get me out of the house. It's fun. You should come with me.

Beryl I don't think so.

Dawn (*after a pause*) So you enjoyed yourself then.

Beryl It was nice to see the sun every day. What's the weather been like here?

Dawn Fantastic. Hottest week on record... Oh ... perhaps I shouldn't have told you that.

Beryl It's marvellous, isn't it? I've just spent three hundred pounds to go abroad and the weather's hotter back home.

Dawn But you haven't got the sea here ... or the Sangria ... or all the young men with their beautiful suntanned bodies.

Beryl looks at her

Not that you'd be at all interested in that kind of thing, of course.

Scott comes in from upstairs. He crosses downstage to the kitchen

Scott I couldn't seem to find a towel in the bathroom. Is it all right if I wash my hands in the kitchen?

Beryl nods and looks at Dawn, whose mouth drops open in surprise

Scott goes out into the kitchen

Beryl touches Dawn's chin in order to close her mouth

Dawn The gardener?

Beryl Yes.

Dawn Dear God.

Beryl There'll come a time in your life when you'll realize that sex isn't everything, Dawn.

Dawn I know ... but it's not now, thank God. Shall I make us a cup of tea? (*She is about to stand*)

Beryl prevents her by holding her arm

Beryl The kettle's boiled once. (*She calls*) Gardener?

Scott (*off*) Yes?

Beryl Would you flick the kettle back on for me, please? (*To Dawn*) Are you going to have him do for you?

Dawn A chance would be a fine thing.

Beryl I only ask because he's almost finished here.

Dawn So better check with Dennis if he still wants it done, you mean?

Beryl shrugs her shoulders

I won't be long. Don't let him out of your sight till I get back.

They both stand

Beryl You're not really attracted to him, are you?

Dawn I'm a woman, Beryl. I've got juices.

Beryl You wouldn't do anything though, would you ... you know ... to wreck your marriage.

Dawn What do you take me for? I've been married to Dennis for fifteen years, Beryl. That's a long time. I mean, I know he's nothing to look at and I know I called him some terrible names just now, but at the end of the day I wouldn't do anything to hurt him.

Beryl So you wouldn't think about committing adultery?

Dawn Oh, I'd *think* about it.

Beryl Would you?

Dawn God yes ... and do ... often ... but not for the last week.

Beryl I'd have thought, if you were going to think about it at all, it would have been during the last week ... you know, with you not speaking to him and that.

Dawn You don't get it, do you? If we're not speaking, then we're not doing anything else. How can I think about doing it with anyone, if I'm not doing it full stop?

Beryl So you do it as well?

Dawn Sorry?

Beryl I've only ever thought about Ted when we're ... you know.

Dawn Really? Oh, you poor thing.

Beryl Don't you think it's wrong to think about someone else?

Dawn Oh, it might be wrong, Beryl ... but it isn't half as bloody boring. Well, you know Dennis ... you've seen him. We'd be there all night if I didn't have my own little fantasy. It doesn't hurt anyone.

Beryl Not even Dennis?

Dawn I don't tell him ... and I don't feel guilty either. He could be pretending I'm Princess Di for all I know.

Beryl I don't think I could do it.

Dawn Well, sometimes needs must, Ber'... Especially after grinding away for twenty minutes. I'm going to have a word with him about the state of our lawn.

Dawn goes out

Beryl (*almost to herself*) I don't think I've lived. (*She sits back down on the settee*)

Scott comes out of the kitchen, carrying two mugs of tea

Scott The kettle boiled. I thought I'd pour.

Beryl looks at Scott's feet

Has everyone gone?
Beryl For the time being.

He moves near and hands her a cup. She looks to his feet before his face

Do you like tea?
Scott Yes.
Beryl Better drink that one, then. (*She means the one in his hand*) I don't like waste. Sit down.
Scott Er no! I'd better not. I'm dirty. I wouldn't want to mark the furniture.

Beryl sips, then looks at Scott's feet again

What is it?
Beryl What?
Scott My feet. You keep looking at my feet.
Beryl Do I? No ... no, I don't think so... (*She takes another sip of tea. Again she can't resist the temptation to look at Scott's feet*)
Scott (*kneeling at the coffee table*) I'm sorry about the confusion...
Beryl The grass needed cutting anyway. (*She gets up and circles the R settee to come and stand behind Scott in order to sneak a look at the nape of his neck*) Everything's been neglected out there. In here too. Everywhere could do with a good lick of paint.
Scott I'm always looking for work. I'm not just a gardener. I can turn my hand to anything. Plumbing, woodwork, decorating, you name it.
Beryl There's enough work here to keep you going till Christmas.
Scott Great. (*He turns and almost catches her looking at his neck*)
Beryl If I could afford you.
Scott I'm very reasonable.
Beryl I think next door want your services.
Scott I can handle that too. Shall I carry on out the garden?
Beryl Yes.
Scott Perhaps you can make a list ... of everything you want done.
Beryl Right.
Scott (*after a pause; standing up*) I'd better get on, then.
Beryl Yes.
Scott I finish around five.
Beryl Fine.
Scott And then I'll be back about half eight.
Beryl Good.
Scott In the morning.

Beryl Of course.
Scott Thanks. (*He pauses*) Is something wrong?
Beryl No.
Scott You seem tense.
Beryl It's just a headache.
Scott (*going to her*) I'm great with headaches.
Beryl Why doesn't that surprise me?
Scott No, really. Can I show you?
Beryl It's all right, I've got a couple of aspirin in my bag.
Scott Please, it won't take a minute. Come here. (*He leads her to the settee* L) Sit down.

She does

Now just hook your legs up over the top.

She is not at all sure about this, so he helps her place her legs over the top of the settee, leaving her head hanging over the seat and resting in his hands

Now, it's all right ... trust me. (*He pauses*) Just relax. You're all right. I'm not going to let you go. (*He begins to massage the back of her neck*) Does that feel good?

She groans a pleasurable reply

Sorry, what was that?

She groans even louder

Suddenly, Angie returns from the front of the house at about the same time as Dawn appears at the french windows

They were both about to say something, but are stunned into silence

Music plays and the Lights fade

CURTAIN

ACT II

SCENE 1

The same. Mid morning, a month later

Music fades and the Lights come up

Scott, wearing white overalls, is painting the outside of the french windows. His radio is on the floor and playing just a little too loudly. A dust sheet and a bag containing a flask and sandwiches are nearby

Beryl comes in from upstairs. She is wearing a housecoat and slippers. Her hair is a mess. They see each other as Beryl moves from R to the R settee, picking up cups

Scott I was going to finish the door, and then I was going to give you a shout.
Beryl What?
Scott Do you know what time it is?
Beryl I don't care.
Scott It's twenty past eleven.
Beryl Did I ask you to come and paint today?
Scott We arranged it yesterday. Are you all right?
Beryl I've been awake since eight o'clock. I just couldn't get out of bed.
Scott You heard me ringing then?
Beryl I heard someone... I hoped they'd go away and thought they had.
Scott I came round the back. I found a key when I moved one of the pots and let myself in.
Beryl (*making for the kitchen*) Do you think you could stop painting... The smell is making me feel sick.

Beryl goes into the kitchen

Scott I could put it all away if you like.
Beryl (*off*) Yes.
Scott Perhaps I can start on something else instead.
Beryl (*off*) No ... I'd rather you didn't work today. I'm not up to it.
Scott Are you sickening for something?

Beryl enters from the kitchen

Beryl You can come again tomorrow … if that's all right.
Scott It's not the flu, is it?
Beryl No, it's not the… Look, do you think you could turn that thing off?

Scott turns off the radio

Thank you. There's nothing wrong with me that a new body wouldn't fix.
Scott There's not much wrong with you physically.
Beryl (*coming to sit on the R settee*) Thank you very much.
Scott There's not. You just need to get motivated. (*He puts the dust sheet down next to the settee and takes out his flask and sandwiches*)
Beryl I'm too old for that sort of thing.
Scott I'm not suggesting you start a serious training programme.
Beryl I'm glad to hear it.
Scott (*offering Beryl a sandwich*) I just think it might be a good idea to start to gently tone up your body.
Beryl It all sounds too much like hard work. (*She shakes her head*)

He returns and sits on the dust sheet. He pauses before pouring two cups of coffee

Scott You want him back, don't you?
Beryl Who?
Scott Your husband.
Beryl What do you know about it?
Scott Not a lot … but I was in the Post Office the other day——
Beryl (*standing up*) I swear to God I'm going to do something to that woman. What did she say?
Scott Not a lot… She just asked if it was right that I was doing some work for you.
Beryl And what did you tell her?
Scott I said "Yes", and she asked what sort of work. She said that she wasn't surprised the place needed some attention … now that your husband had left you for someone else.
Beryl Well, shows how much *she* knows.
Scott (*going to her*) It's not true, then?
Beryl No!

He offers her the coffee and she takes it

Oh, he's left … but according to Angie he's not living with her, he's just lodging there. She's adamant there's nothing going on.

Scott And what do *you* think?

Beryl (*sitting on the coffee table*) I don't know. He insists they're just friends, but... I don't think a man and a woman *can* be friends ... do you?

Scott We're friends, aren't we?

Beryl But you're not living in.

Scott returns to the dust sheet

(*After a pause*) If it *is* friendship like he said, then he's up the creek without a paddle.

Scott Which means?

Beryl Sooner or later he's going to drift down stream.

Scott Where you'll be standing waiting to pull him ashore.

Beryl Not necessarily... There's every possibility he might just wave, of course ... as he slowly goes drifting past.

Scott What will you do then?

Beryl I don't know... I'd rather not think about it.

Scott (*pausing as he lies on the floor on his side*) I'd like to meet him.

Beryl What?

Scott He must be really *something*. You obviously love him a lot. What has he got?

Beryl Nothing very much. Nothing much at all when you think about it.

Scott Is he good-looking?

Beryl Hardly.

Scott Was he ever?

Beryl No, not really.

Scott It's his personality then.

Beryl I don't think he's got one.

Scott I'm serious.

Beryl So am I.

Scott So what's kept you together?

Beryl We're not, or have you forgotten?

Scott I meant for all those years.

Beryl I don't know. You forget how long it's been until you stop and look back. One year just sort of creeps into another and before you know it you're old ... and alone ... and approaching the home stretch. One day you wake up and you realize that three quarters of the things you will do in your life you've done ... and for some that's OK. For others, panic sets in...

Scott And they bolt.

Beryl So be warned. You're young and for you the final furlong is a long way off, but remember what I said. It's much more dignified to grow old gracefully.

Suddenly Beryl has become very serious. They look at each other. They both laugh simultaneously

Scott (*through Beryl's laugh*) Will you let me tone you up?

Beryl (*stopping laughing immediately, then smiling*) You don't know what you're taking on.

Scott Does that mean "Yes"?

Beryl I suppose I could do with losing a couple of pounds.

Scott Great. (*He joins her on the coffee table*) It's not all about weight loss though. (*He turns her away from him and begins to massage her back*) Toning up can make you feel better inside as well as out.

Beryl I hope I know what have I let myself in ... oohh, that's the spot. (*She clearly enjoys the massage*)

Dawn appears at the french windows

Scott Don't worry... I'll be very gentle with you...

Dawn (*just inside the doors*) I bet you say that to all the girls.

Beryl (*surprised*) Dawn! (*She stops Scott continuing*) I didn't hear you coming.

Dawn Obviously.

Scott (*to Dawn*) Careful, I've just painted there.

Dawn (*to Beryl*) Don't tell me now, you're getting up?

Scott She was a bit sluggish this morning.

Dawn Was she?

Beryl Yes. I couldn't even get up to answer the door to Scott.

Scott I had to let myself in the back way.

Dawn (*surprised*) You have a key?

Beryl He found the one I keep under the terracotta pot.

Dawn I see.

Beryl Scott, clear everything away, and then you may as well have the rest of the day off.

Scott I don't mind starting something else.

Beryl No ... you go home and give...

Scott Heather.

Beryl Heather a nice surprise. (*To Dawn*) That's the girlfriend.

Scott Well, if you're sure.

Beryl nods and smiles at him. During the following, he gets all his things together

Dawn I just popped in to see if you were all right and to ask if there was anything I can get you from the shops.

Beryl (*standing up and moving around the back of the L settee*) Are you going to the Post Office?

Dawn I can if you want me to.

Beryl Yes, and you can tell the woman that works there... (*She starts to laugh*)

Scott does too

Oh, never mind, forget it.

Dawn No, go on.

Beryl Just tell her I said to be careful she doesn't catch her tongue in the franking machine.

She and Scott laugh even louder. Scott moves his things up stage

Dawn Are you developing a sense of humour?

Beryl I don't know, am I? I thought I was developing a growing urge to do some serious damage to a certain postal worker. (*Directly to Dawn*) I'm supposed to be receiving my decree nisi any day; it hasn't arrived yet. Perhaps you can ask her if she knows what's happened to it.

Dawn Oh, I'm ever so glad you're making light of it. It's a real move in the right direction.

Beryl Don't get excited... Nothing's really changed. My position is the same, it's Ted who's making all the moves. (*She sits back down on the* R *settee*)

Dawn Maybe, but you're not where you were when he first left. Psychologically you've made huge strides since then.

Beryl Only because I've had you and Angie pushing me on. I still want him... Doesn't that put me back where I started?

Scott No.

They both weren't aware that Scott was listening. They turn to look at him

Sorry. I shouldn't have been listening ... sorry.

Dawn No, it's all right. (*She goes to him*) You agree with me, then?

Scott It's none of my business——

Beryl But?

Scott Don't worry about it. (*He smiles at her*) I'm off now. I'll be round in the morning. Half eight all right?

Beryl nods

Bye.

Scott exits through the french windows

Dawn See you, then. (*She remembers, then calls after him*) Oh, and don't forget you're pruning my corylopsis on Friday. (*In way of an explanation to Beryl*) The winter hazel.

Beryl Are you sure that's not a secret code for, "I'll be waiting for you in the garden shed eleven o'clock on Friday".

Dawn That I should be so lucky. What would a good-looking boy like that want with someone like me?

Beryl A damned sight more than what he'd want with me.

Dawn (*joining Beryl on the settee*) I've been thinking about that.

Beryl What?

Dawn It's time you started doing something to yourself.

Beryl Like what?

Dawn I don't know ... like giving yourself a new look?

Beryl What's the matter with the look I've got?

Dawn It's old.

Beryl I am old.

Dawn You're younger than you dress.

Beryl Am I?

Dawn I recommend a complete make-over, you know, manicures, pedicures, a new hair-style, a complete new wardrobe.

Beryl Hang on a minute ... a new hair-style, you said?

Dawn You've had that look ever since I've known you.

Beryl Your suggestion wouldn't have anything to do with the fact that you need someone to practice on, would it?

Dawn Funnily enough, they do say at the college, if you've got some friends that don't mind doing you a favour...

Beryl You haven't been going there five minutes. What if you make a mess of it?

Dawn I'm very good, Ber'. I cut Dennis' hair last night.

Beryl What's it like?

Dawn Not bad at all... It would have turned out better, but he was snoring and I couldn't concentrate.

Beryl You cut his hair when he was sleeping?

Dawn He wouldn't have let me near him otherwise.

Beryl And you want me to let you loose on mine?

Dawn I did a very good job under the circumstances. Not everyone can cut hair when their subject is stretched out unconscious on the settee.

Beryl If he was sleeping, how did you finish the job?

Dawn I didn't. I thought, he'll get up in a minute to go to the bathroom ... but he didn't. If he had, I'd have moved the cushion, he'd have slept the other way up and I would have finished cutting the rest of his head.

Beryl So he's gone to work this morning with half a haircut?

Dawn Yes.

They both laugh

Well, serve him right, he wouldn't let me go to Spain.

Beryl He's going to love *you*.

Dawn Forget Dennis for a minute ... what about you?

Beryl I know I've let myself go a bit, Dawn ... but I'm not sure I'm ready for *you* yet.

Dawn Oh, please? I know I can do a really nice job.

Beryl (*considering the possibility*) What exactly did you have in mind?

Dawn (*standing up*) Well ... you see all these waves and curls? (*She plays with Beryl's hair*)

Beryl Yes.

Dawn I'd get rid of all them for a start. I think I'd go for something really short.

Beryl I've never had short hair in my life.

Dawn (*getting a chair from up stage and placing it down stage*) That's settled then, it's all coming off.

Beryl What if I don't like it?

Dawn Believe me, Ber', it's going to be just what the doctor ordered.

Beryl Well, I'll think about it.

Dawn Oh no ... if you're going to do it, do it now.

Beryl Have you got the time?

Dawn Yes, of course ... and funnily enough, I just happen to have my scissors on me. (*She holds them up already in her fingers. She places the chair in its final position*) Would you like to take a seat, madam?

Beryl reluctantly sits in the chair. Dawn begins to cut away to her heart's content

Music plays and the Lights fade

Scene 2

Late afternoon the following day. It is quite warm

Music fades and the Lights come up

Scott is again painting the french windows, but inside the room this time

After a moment, Angie comes out of the kitchen with two cans of Coke

Angie Tea-break. (*She throws him a can*) Catch!

Scott Thanks... (*He puts it on the floor*) I'll press on, if it's all right.

Angie Can't wait to rush home, eh?

He doesn't answer

(*She pauses*) So. They've gone shopping, you said.
Scott Left about half nine.
Angie That's a long time for my mother. I hope nothing's wrong.

There is a pause in which Angie steps nearer the windows

You're doing a great job.

He doesn't answer

You have a very nice stroke.
Scott Are you flirting with me?
Angie Would you like it if I was?
Scott I'm not in the mood.
Angie I thought there was *something*.
Scott And there's me thinking I was hiding it so well.

She waits for some sort of reply but there doesn't seem to be one coming. Scott just continues to paint. She gives up and tries to change the subject

Angie My mother tells me you're quite a good carpenter.

Again there is no response

I mentioned that because my front door seems to be sticking. (*She comes more into the room*) I've had a word with the landlord, but you know what they're like. (*She pauses*) I thought perhaps *you* could sort it out ... if you had the time.

There is a pause. Scott puts down his paintbrush and opens his can of Coke

Scott I finished up here early yesterday and your mother gave me the day off. (*He moves to sit on the arm of the* L *settee*) Go home and give Heather a nice surprise, she said... Well, I surprised her all right... Trouble was, I surprised someone else as well.
Angie You mean you caught her at it?
Scott I caught them both at it.
Angie (*standing next to him*) Oh, Scott...
Scott We're supposed to be tying the knot next year... Still, better to find out now, eh?
Angie Oh, you poor thing. Did you throw her out?
Scott Hardly ... it's her flat.

Angie You're not still there?
Scott (*shaking his head*) I slept on a mate's floor last night.
Angie What are you going to do?
Scott I don't know ... find somewhere else quick, I suppose.
Angie (*after a pause*) Why do you think she did it?
Scott (*standing up and crossing* DR) Why does anyone do it?
Angie How long have you been going out with her?
Scott (*sitting on the coffee table*) Since I was seventeen.
Angie Is that when you lost your——
Scott Yes. When did you lose yours?
Angie Would you believe me if I told you I haven't yet?
Scott No.
Angie Twenty-three, then.

They both smile at each other. A pause

What are you going to do about tonight?

He looks at her. She sits next to him

You can't go on sleeping on the floor.
Scott It'll be all right for a day or two.
Angie (*after a pause*) Look, don't take this the wrong way... (*She rests her hand on his leg*) I've got a spare room you can have if you like.
Scott What do you mean, "The wrong way"?
Angie Well, I wouldn't want you to get the wrong idea. (*She moves her hand a little further up his leg*)
Scott (*swallowing*) Like what?
Angie Like I was offering because I had some kind of ulterior motive or something.
Scott But haven't you?
Angie No.
Scott And there's me thinking you wanted to get me in bed.
Angie Well, I don't!
Scott Shame.
Angie Doing anything like that hadn't even entered my head... Why are you smiling?
Scott I like it when you lie.

They both laugh and break away

Angie You're rotten, you are.
Scott (*moving around the back of the coffee table*) Seriously. It's kind of you to offer me a room——

Angie But you're not going to take it.

Scott What about your reputation?

Angie I haven't had one since I was eighteen.

Scott I thought it was twenty-three?

Angie Yes, that's right, twenty-three.

They laugh. A pause

Scott Can I get back to you on it?

Angie (*holding on to the coffee table as she leans back*) You can get whatever you want.

Scott (*after a pause*) The fact is… I'm still reeling a bit. I haven't exactly got my head round what's happened.

Angie You think you might take her back?

Scott I wouldn't have thought so.

Angie But you're not sure?

Scott It's too early to be definite about anything.

Angie That's true.

Scott You know?

Angie I've been there … I must admit I wasn't as controlled about it as you are.

Scott (*sitting on the coffee table again*) You should have seen me yesterday… I lost it completely.

Angie I hope you haven't done anything you regret.

Scott I smashed up the place.

Angie You have a temper, then?

Scott Once in a blue moon. You?

Their lips are inches away from each other

Angie It takes a lot to get me going.

Scott I'll bear it in mind.

They almost kiss

Suddenly, the front door slams

> *Beryl rushes on, followed by Dawn. Both are in summer dresses. Beryl is also wearing a sun hat which covers most of her hair. She places several shopping bags behind the settee*

Beryl Oh my God, my feet are killing me. (*She sees Angie*) How long have *you* been here?

Angie That's a nice welcome.

Beryl No, I didn't expect you. I thought you were coming round tonight.
Dawn I'm parched. Mind if I help myself? (*She takes the can out of Scott's hand and all but empties it*) I've never been so thirsty.
Angie (*offering her can*) Mum?
Beryl No, I'm going to have a cup of tea. (*To Scott*) How have you been getting on?
Scott I've finished the outside.
Beryl Good. I hope *she* hasn't been hindering you?
Angie I haven't been here *that* long.
Beryl (*giving her a look*) I've got *your* number.
Angie (*insisting*) I haven't. Scott, tell her.
Scott Half an hour, tops. I'll put the kettle on.

Scott goes off into the kitchen

Beryl (*inspecting the paintwork*) He's doing a nice job... He can start on the bathroom next.
Dawn (*sitting on the arm of the L settee*) It's good you're taking an interest. Six weeks ago you wouldn't have cared if the house crumbled around your feet.
Beryl My heart's still not totally in it.
Dawn No, we know where *your* heart is, don't we, Ang'?
Angie I heard a little whisper yesterday.
Beryl I'm not sure I want to hear it.
Angie It might not even be true.
Beryl If it's about your father, the less I hear these days, the better.
Angie But you ought to know.
Beryl Sometimes ignorance is the best thing.
Angie I'll keep it to myself, then.
Beryl Yes. I'm better off in the dark. Chances are it'll only upset me anyway.
Angie Oh, it's not bad news or anything.
Beryl (*sitting on the R settee*) It's not? What is it then?
Angie You just said you didn't want to know.
Beryl I've changed my mind. Come on, tell me and put me out of my misery.
Angie Well, like I said, I don't know whether it's true or not, but ... apparently he's taking early retirement.
Beryl Your father? I don't believe it. You've got to be old to retire and he'd never own up to that.
Angie Well, that's what I've heard. He's getting a nice big fat handshake too ... which is why I thought you should know.
Dawn (*sitting next to Beryl*) Yes, by law you're entitled to half... Mind you, saying that, if me and Dennis ever split up he'd probably let me have it all... The only thing he'd fight custody over is the settee.
Beryl Men ... they're all the same.

Angie Well, no ... not all. (*She looks out towards the kitchen*)
Dawn I suppose there's an exception to every rule.

Dawn and Angie give each other a wicked look

Beryl (*getting her shopping from behind the settee*) When you two have
stopped drooling... (*To Angie*) I'll show you my new wardrobe.
Angie You're going to have to be quick, then. I'm going swimming in half
an hour.
Dawn And I'd better go too. (*She makes to leave through the french
windows*)
Beryl Oh, Dawn?

Dawn stops and puts her hand on the paintwork

Thanks for coming with me.
Dawn Anytime, you know that. (*She almost turns to leave again*)
Angie Oh, and Dawn?

Dawn stops

The paint's wet.

*Dawn looks at her hand as she peels her fingers away from the woodwork.
She holds up her hand and makes a face as she shows it to the others. She
runs off down the garden*

Go on then ... make me jealous and show me all you've bought.
Beryl Well... (*She takes a dress out of one of the bags*) I wasn't really sure
about this, but it was a bargain and Dawn said she liked it. (*She takes the
dress and holds it up against her*) What do you think?
Angie Difficult to tell with that silly hat on. Take it off.
Beryl It's not silly.
Angie It is with that dress. Take it off.
Beryl I like it.
Angie I'm sure you do, but you're indoors now, you don't need to wear it.
Beryl But I *want* to wear it.
Angie Why?
Beryl About the dress...
Angie About the hat.
Beryl The colours are nice, don't you think?
Angie What have you done?
Beryl What do you mean?
Angie (*raising her voice a little*) Show me what you've done!

A pause. Reluctantly, Beryl slowly takes off her hat to reveal her new short haircut. There is a pause between them as Angie steps nearer to take a closer look

Beryl What do you think?

For a while Angie doesn't answer

Angie I think it's stunning.
Beryl You do?
Angie Who did it for you?
Beryl Dawn, would you believe.
Angie It's fantastic.
Beryl It takes a bit of getting used to.
Angie I love it.
Scott (*off*) Are you having tea, Angie?

Beryl rushes to put the hat back on, but Angie grabs it before her and tosses it on the settee

(*Off*) Angie?
Angie (*calling to him*) Er ... no. I'm going in a minute.
Beryl It doesn't make me look too young, does it?
Angie It makes you look wonderful.
Beryl Are you sure?
Angie Don't take *my* word for it. Ask Scott what *he* thinks ... although I'm not sure he'd be the right person to ask at the moment.
Beryl Why?
Angie Ask him to tell you about it. I'm going to go now.
Beryl Ask him to tell me about what?
Angie I don't think you did him any favours when you sent him home early yesterday ... although for a minute I thought you did me a big one.
Beryl What are you talking about?
Angie He's moved out. (*She calls to him*) Bye, Scott.
Scott (*off*) See you.
Angie I'll probably ring later ... if not, I'll call round in the morning. Ta-rah.

Angie goes out

There is a pause. Beryl picks up the dress and again holds it against her body, looking down at it and swaying back and forth

Scott comes out of the kitchen, carrying two cups of tea

Immediately she sees him, she flings the dress back on the settee

Scott Your kettle was playing up so I had to fiddle with… (*He looks up and sees her*)

They stare at each other for a moment

Beryl What?
Scott (*standing perfectly still*) What have you done?
Beryl (*after a pause*) Oh, the hair, you mean? You don't like it?
Scott (*a smile growing across his face*) It's very nice.
Beryl You're not just saying that?
Scott No … it's so different … it's great. (*After a pause, he hands her her tea*)
Beryl (*taking it*) Oh … thanks. (*She sips*)

There is another pause

What was Angie going on about?

He shakes his head slightly

She said something about, you've moved out.
Scott Oh that, yes … well…
Beryl Is it true?

He nods

Because I gave you the day off? I don't understand.
Scott You did me a favour, that's all.

She looks at him for more of an explanation

Heather didn't expect me. Best laid plans… Do I have to spell it out?
Beryl (*not understanding his situation for a moment; then she gets it*) Oh, I'm sorry…
Scott (*returning to the french windows and the painting*) Don't be … it was hardly your fault.
Beryl I still feel partly responsible. You must be terribly hurt.

He doesn't answer

Forget the work for today.
Scott No! I'd rather I didn't… Helps keep my mind occupied, you know?

Beryl Where are you staying?

Scott At a mate's for now.

Beryl Well, not any more, you can stay here with me.

Scott No, really.

Beryl It's ridiculous. I have all these bedrooms——

Scott You don't have to do this.

Beryl I want to.

Scott But you live on your own.

Beryl Yes.

Scott (*after a pause*) What will people say?

Beryl (*after a pause*) Of course … yes, silly of me. I'm sorry, I wasn't thinking of you.

Scott Neither was I. I don't give a damn what people think about me … it's *you* I was concerned about. (*He pauses*) Look, it's very kind of you to offer and I appreciate your concern … but for your sake I think it's best I say "No", don't you?

There is a pause as she considers this

Beryl Well … whatever.

Scott I haven't offended you?

Beryl No.

Scott That's the last thing I'd want.

Beryl Let's forget I mentioned it.

Scott Oh, I couldn't do that. It meant a lot.

Beryl (*after a pause*) This is silly. You need somewhere to stay and I need someone to care for … you know, tend to. Cook and clean for.

Scott (*after a pause*) Well … when you put it like that it seems silly not to help each other out. Agreed?

Beryl Agreed.

They toast each other with their cups of tea. There is a pause in which Beryl sets down her cup and begins to collect together her shopping

Scott I can't imagine what Angie will say… She did ask me first.

Beryl Did she?

He nods

(*Putting the dress in the bag*) Well, she would have, I suppose. Stay with her, then. I've told you, it's no big thing … just as long as you've got a decent bed to sleep in. (*She pauses*) Of course, you will have to keep your door locked there, which is something you won't have to worry about in this house.

Scott (*smiling*) What are you suggesting?

Beryl You know very well that she likes you. She knows her way around, that girl. Believe me, she'll be in your bed and under your sheets before you've had time to take your socks off.

Scott You're being very naughty.

Beryl She's a good girl and for all I know an opportunity like that might be exactly what you're waiting for… Personally, I'd have thought you were too raw for anything like that at the moment … but, I could be wrong of course.

Scott (*playfully*) I think I'd better get back to work.

Beryl (*smiling*) In other words, "Mind my own business".

Scott That's not what I meant…

There is a pause as they look at each other

All right if I move some things in later on?

Beryl Fine … fine.

He nods and half smiles before returning to his paint pots. Beryl smiles as she rams the hat into one of the shopping bags

Music plays and the Lights fade

SCENE 3

A month later. Early evening

Music fades and the Lights come up. The curtains to the french windows are closed. There are a few table lamps on

Angie is lounging on the settee reading a magazine. Eventually she tosses it to her side and checks the time by her watch. She sighs. Someone knocks on the outside of the french windows

Angie opens the curtains wide to see and lets Dawn in

Dawn It's only me.

Angie Come in.

Dawn I wanted a word with your mother, but I didn't know she had company.

Angie (*sitting on the R settee*) She hasn't … well, not mine anyway… I'm here on my own.

Dawn (*surprised*) Oh.

Angie I thought I'd pop over, seeing as we haven't spoken for a couple of days.

Dawn She's out, then?

Angie Unless she's hiding somewhere from me.

Dawn Why would she do that?

Angie I wasn't serious, Dawn.

Dawn gives a little embarrassed smile

Dawn Are you all right, you sound a bit——

Angie What?

Dawn Well, you know.

Angie Sorry?

Dawn Scratchy.

Angie (*scratchy*) I don't know ... do I?

Dawn (*pausing slightly before joining Angie on the settee*) If you're worried about your mother——

Angie Worried? Why should I be worried? It appears she's doing remarkably well when you consider how depressed she was a couple of months ago.

Dawn But that's good, isn't it?

Angie Apparently she even goes swimming now.

Dawn Yes, isn't that wonderful?

Angie You know about it then?

Dawn It was *I* who coaxed her to go.

Angie But you don't go with her.

Dawn No, I don't like the water myself.

Angie She was even seen coming out of a health shop the other day.

Dawn I think that might have been Scott's influence.

Angie I'm sure it was.

Dawn Did you know he's a vegetarian?

Angie (*almost shouting*) No, I didn't!

Dawn He's a lovely boy... He and your mother get on like a house on... Oh dear, is that what it is? Are you afraid she's getting involved with someone half her age?

Angie Well, isn't she?

Dawn I don't think so. I know the word is out that he's her toy boy, but I don't believe it... Do you?

Angie She's very vulnerable at the moment... So is he.

Dawn True. Well, when you put it like that, it's not unthinkable they've found comfort in each other's arms.

Angie (*getting up and moving behind the settee*) Yes it is, change the subject.

Dawn No, seriously. Whether they're just good friends or not... I think he's

been marvellous for her, don't you? She's practically a new woman since
he moved in.

Angie She hasn't been spending much time in the house, I know that.

Dawn I know you're her daughter, Angie, and I understand your concern ...
but you sound just that teensy weensy bit jealous to me.

Angie (*firmly*) Did you want something?

Dawn Pardon?

Angie When you came in. I presume you wanted something.

Dawn Oh yes ... a magazine. Your mother said I could borrow it.

Angie Which one?

Dawn I'm not sure. She said there was an article in it about a woman who'd
had her jaws wired.

Angie That's an excellent idea. When are you going to have it done? (*She
begins to look for the magazine under the cushions*)

Dawn (*laughing*) It's not for me, silly, it's for Dennis. He's so big now,
physical exercise isn't practical. Getting him wired up seems to be the only
option.

Angie I don't know why you don't go the whole hog and plug him in while
you're at it.

Dawn laughs

Beryl and Scott are seen briefly outside the french windows jogging from
R *to* L

I'm serious.

Dawn That's what I like about you ... always good for a laugh.

Angie I don't know what she's done with it. You're going to have to wait
till she gets back.

The kitchen door slams and voices are heard off

Dawn (*moving up stage*) I won't have to wait long by the sound of it.

Dawn stands C

Beryl runs in, wearing a jogging suit. She immediately collapses on the L
settee

*Scott follows her into the room similarly dressed. He has a small towel
around his neck, which he takes, and standing behind the settee, fans
Beryl's face*

Scott (*to Angie*) Give her a minute to get her breath back.

Angie What have you done to her? My mother has never been jogging in her life.
Scott Not true. We've been twice a week for the past fortnight.
Angie You'll kill her.
Scott She'll be fine.
Angie What with the swimming and the jogging——
Scott She does aerobics too. She's really getting into shape.
Angie You'll be telling me next she's a veggie like you.
Scott I'm working on it.
Angie And what else are you working on?
Scott Sorry?
Angie What are you doing to her?
Scott What do you mean?
Angie Look at her, for God's sake. She can't keep up with you.
Scott I'm not pushing her.
Angie She's fifty-nine.
Beryl (*snatching the towel from her face*) Fifty-eight!
Angie (*to Beryl*) It's your birthday next week. (*To Scott*) She's no spring chicken.
Beryl (*getting up and checking herself in the mirror*) You speak for yourself. I feel better than I have in years.
Angie You keep this up and you'll be dropping dead.
Beryl I'm enjoying myself.
Angie It's too much for you.
Beryl Says who?
Scott I keep a careful eye on her.
Angie I bet you do.
Beryl (*to Angie*) What's it to do with you anyway?
Angie I'll tell you what it's to do with me——
Scott (*crossing along the back on his way to the hall*) I'm going to have a shower.
Angie If you can wait for the two of us to go I'm sure she'll join you.
Scott What?
Angie You heard.
Beryl Angie, you'd better go *now*.
Scott Look, let me explain——
Beryl You don't have to explain anything to anyone. Go and have your shower.
Angie No, let him talk. I'd like to hear what he's got to say.
Beryl He's not answerable to you and neither am I.
Scott (*to Angie*) You haven't got anything to worry about.
Angie You're not standing in *my* shoes.
Scott They wouldn't fit me.

Angie That's a terrible joke.

Scott I know. Look, let me freshen up ... then we can all calm down and talk about this rationally. OK?

She doesn't answer

OK?

She nods her head once ever so slightly

Scott turns and leaves

There is a pause

Beryl I don't know what you think you're playing at.

Angie Shouldn't that be *my* line?

Beryl You've got a nerve.

Angie Can't you see what's happening?

Beryl The trouble with you is you've been spending too much time in the Post Office.

Angie I don't have to listen to gossip, I can see it first hand myself.

Beryl What do you see, then?

Angie You want me to spell it out for you?

Beryl Yes, go on.

Angie (*after a pause*) I see an overweight, late middle-aged woman, who has become so infatuated with a young good-looking stud that she's quite prepared to make a fool of herself. I mean, just look at you... My mother's going swimming and jogging, it's absurd.

Beryl Your mother is feeling great and she's happy... If that's absurd, then you're going to have to live with it.

Angie What's happening to you? You've changed.

Beryl Yes I have, thank God ... and hopefully I'll go on changing. You're quite right, I am infatuated with him ... but not in the way *you* think. Yes, he fascinates me. He's taught me things, and what's more he makes me laugh. It would have been nice if you thought I deserved a bit of that. (*She pauses*) Shall I tell you what *I* see? I see a daughter who wants something, and she's afraid her mother is going to get it before her. It's ridiculous. What I want from Scott and what you want from him are two entirely different things. The sooner you realize that the better. If anyone is making a fool of herself here, I don't think it's me, do you?

Angie (*after a pause*) *Have* I made a fool of myself?

Dawn Well, only to me.

They both turn around to see Dawn. Each had forgotten she was there

Angie Oh... Dawn! I'd forgotten you were here. (*She pauses*) I'm all embarrassed now. (*To Beryl*) I'm sorry.

Beryl It would be nice if you said it to my "lodger", too.

Angie (*making to leave*) I'll do it now.

Beryl He's in the bathroom.

Angie I can tell him through the door... You never know, he might ask me in.

Dawn If he does, call me... I wouldn't mind a quick shower myself.

Angie You get lost... You've got your own fella.

Dawn (*laughing*) There's no room for me to shower with Dennis even if I wanted too.

Angie leaves to go upstairs

(*To Beryl*) It's true ... we've had to dismantle the cubicle. If he gets any bigger he'll have to go to the car-wash. (*She sits on the* L *settee as she remembers something*) Which is why I'm here. I thought I'd show him that article in your magazine. I'm going to try and talk him into having his jaws wired.

Beryl I can't remember what I've done with it. (*She begins to look, checking under the* R *and* L *settee cushions*)

Dawn Angie's had a quick look, but she couldn't put her hands on it either. The situation's desperate now... Dennis is seriously overweight.

Beryl I hope I haven't thrown it out.

Dawn Oh, well, if you have, I'll just have to get a metal coat hanger and do it myself.

They both laugh. Beryl continues to look

Beryl (*looking under the coffee table*) It might not *be* his eating habits, you know. It's quite possible it's his glands... Have you thought of that? (*She flicks through a magazine*)

Dawn I've thought of everything. At the end of the day it's got to be what he's putting in his mouth. (*She pauses*) There's no truth in it, then?

Beryl In what?

Dawn What's going around.

Beryl (*covering a smile*) About me and Scott?

Dawn nods

What do *you* think ... or better still, what does the woman in the Post Office think?

Dawn Oh, well, she's telling everyone you're selling up and going to live abroad with him.

Beryl So I'm emigrating now, am I? You know, it always amazes me where all these rumours come from.

Dawn Well, I think that one started from the fact that he went in there to buy a passport.

Beryl stops flicking through the magazine then tosses it down on the coffee table

Beryl I'll look for it later, Dawn. Perhaps I've taken it upstairs.

Dawn Are you all right?

Beryl Of course I am. Why shouldn't I be?

Dawn (*after a pause*) You didn't know, did you?

Beryl That he bought a passport? It's none of my business. He's obviously planning on going away somewhere… It doesn't mean he's not coming back… Everybody's entitled to a holiday.

Dawn That's what *I* said.

Beryl Did you?

Dawn He's very special to you, isn't he?

Beryl He's helped me a lot… He's changed my life, really.

Dawn Don't give him all the credit… You had something to do with it too.

Beryl (*after a pause*) Nothing good goes on for ever. When the time comes, I'm just going to have to let him go.

Dawn Not without a fight, I hope.

Beryl I read once, that sometimes the only way of keeping someone … is to set them free.

Dawn In a magazine?

Beryl I think so.

Dawn I'll borrow that as well, then, if you can find it.

They both laugh but it fades almost immediately

Beryl Enjoy things while they last, that's my motto. Sooner or later something always comes along and bursts the bubble.

Dawn You're lucky you've had a bubble to burst. Nothing as exciting as Scott has ever happened to me…

Beryl Funnily enough I wasn't talking about Scott.

Dawn …except in my head, of course.

Beryl (*after a pause*) You still do that? (*She stands in front of the* R *settee*)

Dawn Occasionally. We don't do it often these days, as I'm sure you've noticed.

Beryl No, I hadn't realized. I thought Dennis had finally moved the bed away from the wall.

Dawn He couldn't move it now even if he wanted to. His body movements have become far too restricted. Having sex these days is a bit like travelling on Le Shuttle … we just roll on and roll off.

Beryl Is he happy?

She doesn't answer

You really should be helping him as much as you can.

Dawn Why do you think I'm in here for the magazine?

Beryl You're going to have to do more than that. He's going to need all the support he can get.

Dawn I agree. There'll come a time when his legs will never take all that weight.

Beryl I'm serious. I'm going to make sure you're behind him all the way.

Dawn He's so big, Beryl, if I stood behind him, you wouldn't know I was there.

Beryl It's not funny.

Dawn I'm not laughing.

Beryl I don't think it's all *his* fault.

Dawn What?

Beryl You've been too soft with him … done too much. Getting him wired up isn't the answer, Dawn. If you're going to help him, you've got to start by teaching him to help himself.

Dawn How am I going to do that?

Beryl I don't know … but it's something to think about.

Angie comes in from the hall and sits on the arm of the R settee

Everything all right?

Angie Fine. He said he thought we should go out on Friday … have a meal together.

Beryl That'll confuse things at the Post Office.

There is a knock at the front door

Angie I'll get it.

Angie goes out

A pause. Beryl looks at Dawn, who seems to be in a world of her own

Beryl Dawn?

Dawn (*coming out of it*) What?

Beryl You were miles away.

Dawn You're right, you know. I should never have let him get the size he is.

Beryl Look, I know I said it's not all his fault, but I didn't mean most of it was yours either.

Dawn But I'm all he's got. I wish I knew what to do.

Beryl You'll think of something. Just remember that sometimes you have to be cruel to be kind.

Angie returns from the hall

Angie Mum? You've got a visitor. (*She steps inside the room*)

Ted follows her in. His dress has a younger look about it, and he is wearing a toupee

Beryl Oh...

Ted (*after a pause*) I wondered if I could have a word.

There is rather a long pause in which all three women notice the toupee and share looks. Angie makes the first move

Angie (*trying not to laugh*) Right ... well. I'm just going upstairs.

Angie's control disappears as she goes through the door

Another awkward pause

Dawn (*trying not to laugh*) Did you hear that?

Beryl What?

Dawn It's Dennis. I'm sure he called. (*She pauses*) I'd better go. (*She pauses*) Now. (*She pauses*) Had I better go now?

Beryl Well, if Dennis called...

Dawn Yes. Right. Well, I'll be off then.

Dawn eventually goes off via the french windows shaking with almost uncontrollable laughter

There is a very awkward pause. Beryl and Ted look at each other

Music plays and the Lights fade

SCENE 4

A few days later. Early evening

Music fades and the Lights come up

Dawn is standing UL

Scott is standing DC *in front of the coffee table. On the floor and at his feet is a bag containing hand weights. He is flexing his arm muscles with two dumb-bells. Dawn's gaze is sheer unadulterated lust. Scott wears a faint smile. He is aware of her look burning into the back of his head*

A pause

Scott Are you *sure* you won't have a drink?
Dawn (*swallowing*) Absolutely.
Scott I hate drinking by myself.
Dawn It doesn't bother me.
Scott You do drink, then?
Dawn Occasionally.
Scott But not tonight.
Dawn No.
Scott Fair enough. (*Suddenly, he reaches out, flexing his muscles by holding the dumb-bells left and right*)
Dawn (*immediately*) I'll have a vodka tonic.

Scott smiles and places the weights back in his bag. He takes the bag and places it on the floor next to the drinks cabinet. He pours two drinks. Dawn sits on the L *settee*

I'm not staying. I only popped in to see how she looks.
Scott She's going to look great.
Dawn Oh, I know that... I just wanted to see her, that's all... You know what we women are like. (*She pauses*) How is she up there? Nervous as a kitten, I expect.
Scott Actually, she's quite calm ... or cool is a better word.
Dawn Good... The last thing we want is for Ted to think she's throwing herself at him.

A pause in which Scott hands Dawn her drink. He moves behind the settee, walking around the back of it before coming to sit next to her

You can tell me to mind my own business if you like … but what's going to happen to you? If she takes him back. I mean, you must have thought about it.

Scott (*sitting down*) Oh, I've got plans.

Dawn (*after a pause*) I was ever so sorry to hear about you and your fiancé.

Scott (*quite determinedly*) She wasn't my fiancé.

Dawn No! Quite. Right. (*She pauses*) Well, I was ever so sorry anyway. (*She pauses again*) She's very fond of you, you know.

Scott Heather?

Dawn No, Beryl. Whatever happens between her and Ted, I'm sure she'll see that you're all right.

Scott (*leaning back and towards her slightly on the settee*) I'm big enough to take care of myself.

Dawn Yes… I'm sure you are.

A pause

Do you think she'll take him back?

Scott I don't know.

Dawn *I* think she will.

Scott That's assuming he's coming here to ask her, of course.

Dawn You think he's coming to ask her for something else?

Scott You were here when he called. Apparently all he wanted was a word… It could be about anything.

Dawn In that case, do you think she'll be all right? What I mean is, should we leave her on her own with him. I could keep an eye on her, you know, because I don't think she's as stable as she makes out.

Scott I think she'll be fine. You're probably right. Chances are he *does* want to move back in … and I think *she* wants him to as well, otherwise she wouldn't be upstairs now making herself look good.

Dawn It'll be wasted on him.

Scott What's he like?

Dawn He's a funny little man, really. Not the sort you'd think would up and leave at *his* age. (*She pauses*) He wears platform shoes and a toupee. He must be all of five foot two in his stocking feet and he drives a BMW and you know what they say about little men with big cars… (*She laughs*) I don't know what she sees in him. Why do you want to know?

Scott I don't really.

Angie appears in the hall doorway

Angie Are you ready for this?

Dawn gets up and steps backwards slightly

Angie steps aside to let Beryl into the room. She is looking very elegant, stunning even. She is a total transformation of the woman we saw at the start of the play

Angie is smiling like a Cheshire cat and Scott and Dawn are speechless. A long pause

Beryl Well, somebody say *something*.
Dawn You look gorgeous… Doesn't she, Scott?

Scott nods and smiles

I can't believe it's you.
Angie Well, let's hope my father can. (*She takes the glasses from Scott and Dawn and returns them to the cabinet*)
Beryl What time is it?
Angie You've got ten minutes yet.
Dawn Unless he comes early.
Beryl In which case perhaps you'd all better leave.
Scott I just need to pop upstairs. (*To Angie*) Are you ready?
Angie Whenever *you* are.

Scott leaves the room

Dawn (*to Angie*) You're both going out?
Angie (*going to the mirror*) He's taking me for a meal.
Dawn Don't talk about food … we're both on diets in our house.
Beryl Dennis didn't… "go" for the jaw job then.
Dawn When he saw the photograph in the magazine he said he'd rather have his stomach stapled; but that's irreversible, so he's giving a diet a one last go.
Beryl How's he doing?
Dawn He thinks he's doing fine, but he ate two pound of tomatoes before I came in here.
Angie At least he's trying.
Dawn Where's he taking you, somewhere nice?
Angie I don't know … probably.
Dawn I expect so … and then when you least expect it, he'll ask you.
Angie Ask me what?
Dawn If he hasn't already of course.
Angie What are you talking about?
Dawn (*after a pause, in which she realizes she has spoken too soon*) Nothing. Forget I said anything.

Angie looks at Beryl, but she avoids her gaze

Angie (*smiling*) What's going on?

No-one answers

Does somebody know something *I* don't?

Dawn (*after a pause*) I'm going in now... (*She turns to leave, then stops and turns back into the room*) Don't forget, if you need me, I'm only next door.

Beryl Why would I need you?

Dawn Well ... things might not go exactly as you want them. I just want you to know that I'm not far away ... should anything go wrong. (*She turns, then remembers something*) Oh ... you look stunning, Ber' ... Ted's in for a real shock.

Dawn leaves through the french windows

Angie What's she on about?

Beryl I think she's afraid your father might get violent.

Angie I didn't mean that, I meant about me and Scott.

Beryl (*shrugging*) I don't know. Unless it's to do with the passport.

Angie What passport?

Beryl Scott's. He's renewed it. She's got it in her head he's going to ask you to go away with him.

Angie (*pouring herself a drink at the cabinet*) Do you think he might?

Beryl It's possible.

Angie But he hasn't mentioned it to you.

Beryl He doesn't tell me everything.

Angie Maybe he will, then.

Beryl I know I've seen you in action, but it is only the first time you're going out with him.

Angie Meaning?

Beryl Meaning it's a bit much to hope for on your first date.

Angie Yes, well, like you said, you've seen me in action. (*She pauses*) Has he said anything about me, you know, in passing?

Beryl We don't have those sort of conversations.

Angie So what do you talk about?

Beryl Lots of things. His work, his hobbies, the television, alternative medicine ... he's well into that.

Angie What about his family?

Beryl If I tell you everything you'll have nothing to talk about.

Angie You can give me *something* to bring up, or better still, is there anything I should avoid, like, divorce or religion or something?

Beryl I wouldn't worry about it. I can't imagine for a minute that either of you will be stuck for something to say.

Angie Just like you and Dad later, then.

Beryl Oh, I don't plan on saying much. I thought I'd play the listener tonight.

Angie (*after a pause*) I wonder why he wants a word.

Beryl (*crossing to the mirror*) Probably wants to make arrangements ... discuss settlement, that sort of thing.

Angie Do you think he wants to sell the house?

Beryl He's not going to want me to stay here forever.

Angie What will you do?

Beryl Buy him out. My half of things should cover it.

Angie Wouldn't you like something smaller?

Beryl Not really. It's been my home for thirty odd years... I'm quite happy here.

Angie Are you, Mum ... happy?

A pause. Suddenly, there is a knock on the front door

You haven't answered me.

Beryl That's probably your father... Go and open the door.

Angie (*after a pause*) Are you ready for this?

Beryl I think I'm ready for anything.

There is a pause before Angie turns and leaves

Immediately she has gone, Beryl closes the curtains and goes to the drinks cabinet to pour herself a drink. She stands at the cabinet

Ted (*off*) I didn't expect anyone else to be here.

Angie (*off*) Don't worry, I'm not staying.

Ted comes into the room, followed by Angie

Ted It's just that I need to speak to her alone.

Angie I'm just on my way out.

Ted sees someone standing at the cabinet. He looks a little puzzled. After a moment or two he calls her

Ted (*not at all sure*) Beryl?

Beryl pauses for a moment before turning round to face him

(*After a pause*) I er... I wasn't sure——

Beryl Sure it was me? It's all right, I took some convincing too. Drink?
Ted Er, no.
Beryl (*sitting on the arm of the* R *settee*) Very wise ... best to keep a clear
head. I'll just have the one myself.
Ted How long have you looked like that?
Angie (*to Ted*) It suits her, doesn't it?
Ted (*to Angie*) She looks so... (*He looks at Beryl*) You look totally different.
Beryl You too. It's still me, Ted. It's just a new frock and hair-do, that's all.
Ted I think I *will* have a drink.
Beryl (*going to him as she walks a circle on her way to the drinks cabinet*)
I see you've done something with your hair as well.
Angie (*scornfully*) Mum!
Beryl Oh, I'm sorry, you're not supposed to mention it, are you? Oh, well,
it's done now. At least we've got it out of the way, so there's no need to
bring it up again. (*She pours him a drink*)
Angie (*after a pause; to Ted*) I think it looks all right.
Ted Do you?

She nods

If you didn't know me, would you be able to tell? (*He stands dummy-like
with his head held slightly forward*) The truth now.
Beryl Of course she can tell. I'm not being funny, Ted, but I can see the join
from here.
Ted You shouldn't ... it was very expensive.
Beryl (*handing him his drink*) How much?
Ted Five hundred pounds.

Beryl crosses to the bureau and writes something down

What are you doing?
Beryl Just making a note; you never know, I might need to refer to it later.

Ted takes a sip

Scott comes in from the hallway

Ted almost chokes

Scott (*to Angie*) OK then?
Beryl Have you got your key, Scott?
Scott Yes, but I thought I wouldn't come home tonight.

Angie can't believe her ears and beams at her mother

It'll give you some privacy.

Beryl Nonsense. Me and Ted will be through by ten.

Scott You take all the time you need.

Angie Yes.

Scott I've made arrangements to stay out … after I've taken Angie home, of course.

Angie It's all right, Scott… I'm my own woman. You haven't got to put up a pretence for my parents.

Scott I wasn't… I really *have* arranged to sleep somewhere else.

Angie tries to say several different things, but nothing comes out of her mouth. Her face is a picture. Scott now realizes she had other ideas and decides to make a sharp exit

Shall we go then?

Scott goes, leaving Angie gob-smacked and rooted to the spot

Beryl Angie?

She seems to come round

Are you going?

Stunned, Angie turns and follows Scott off

There is a pause

Ted So it's true then … you really do have him living here.

Beryl Yes. Do you want another one of those? (*She means the drink*)

He shakes his head

Ted Is Angie seeing him?

Beryl They're going for a meal.

Ted *We* could have done that.

Beryl What, and be seen out together?

Ted It's not late, we can still book.

Beryl Why would you want to take me out? (*She answers him before he has the chance to reply*) Oh yes, I get it, "Neutral ground". (*She sits on the arm of the* L *settee*) No, I'd rather stay here in the security of my own four walls, thank you very much.

Ted (*after a pause*) How long has it been going on … with him and Angie?

Beryl I'm not sure there is anything "going on". They're being polite and making themselves scarce.

Ted Together.
Beryl Angie likes him... I don't know if it's going to lead to anything.
Ted Why? Is he involved with someone else?
Beryl I don't know... (*She sips her drink*) It's possible.

There is a pause in which they stare at each other

Are you sure you won't have another drink?
Ted Do you want to get me drunk?
Beryl I don't think I've got enough whisky for that.
Ted (*after a pause*) How are you?
Beryl *I'm* going to have another one anyway. (*She moves* DC)
Ted I'll join you, then.

She stops, turns and takes his glass

Have you been all right?
Beryl (*heading for the drinks cabinet*) I understand you're retired now.
Ted Yes.
Beryl All that spare time, and all that money ... well, half of all that money.
(*She pours two more drinks*) You understand I'm entitled to half.
Ted (*sitting on the* L *settee*) Do we *have* to talk about that?
Beryl Isn't that why you're here?
Ted No, not really.

There is a pause

Beryl When you turned up the other day and asked to have a word, my
immediate reaction was to say "No".
Ted You *did* say "No".
Beryl I know ... but as Angie said, how am I going to sort out my financial
situation if I refuse to talk to you?
Ted So that's why you changed your mind.
Beryl That's why you're sitting here now, yes.
Ted I thought——
Beryl What?
Ted (*shaking his head*) This is going to be harder than I thought.
Beryl (*handing him his glass*) Perhaps this will make it easier.

He takes it, drinks it in one, then begins to wander around the room

Ted You're very strong.
Beryl What?

Ted And different. There's something hard about you.
Beryl Knock for knock. Life makes you like that. By "life" I mean you, of course.
Ted I know I've hurt you.
Beryl You've no idea how much.
Ted I'd like to make it up to you.
Beryl And why would you want to do that?
Ted Will you sit down?
Beryl What?
Ted Please ... sit down?

There is a pause before she obliges. She sits on the R *settee*

Beryl Now, are you going to tell me some earth-shattering news, or do you just want to feel taller than me?
Ted (*after a pause*) You have every right to be bitter.
Beryl I'm not bitter.
Ted What I did to you was unforgivable.
Beryl Everybody thought so.
Ted I'm not trying to make excuses for myself——
Beryl That's all right, then.
Ted (*edging away* DL) But I was going through some sort of "thing".
Beryl I told you that at the time.
Ted I know you did ... but because of the nature of what I was going through, you were the last person I could turn to.
Beryl And the woman in accounts was the first.
Ted I don't expect you to understand——
Beryl But I do.
Ted (*surprised*) Do you?
Beryl Oh yes. I didn't like it then, and I don't agree with it now ... but I understood it. Is she still married?
Ted Of course.
Beryl I hope the three of you will be very happy together.
Ted I don't live there anymore.
Beryl Since when?
Ted (*sitting on the* L *settee*) About a month.
Beryl Do they know at the Post Office?
Ted What sort of a question is that?
Beryl A silly one. So where are you living these days?
Ted I've got a flat ... it's not much ... it's above a newsagent's. (*He pauses*) I've come here tonight to ask you something. I know I've probably blown it, but, it's got to be worth a try.
Beryl You want me to take you back.

Ted I want you to think about it.

Beryl I knew this day would come.

Ted Will you? Think about it?

Beryl Through all the dark bits, the tears, the crying myself to sleep, I said one day it would happen. Every day I told myself it would happen.

Ted Please?

Beryl Until a couple of months ago. Suddenly, I didn't think about it all the time. Suddenly twenty-four hours had passed without your name popping into my head. (*She pauses as she gets up and moves down stage*) A day turned to two days and two days to a week ... before I knew it I had a life of my own ... a life without you...

Ted Please.

Beryl And I liked it. Leaving me like you did was hardly fair ... asking to come back is almost cruel.

Ted You won't consider it, then?

Beryl I never said that.

Ted So what *are* you saying? Do I have a chance?

Beryl (*after a pause*) You've told me why you left ... you haven't said why you want to come back.

Ted I made a mistake. I know I don't deserve it, but I want a second chance.

Beryl Why?

Ted I don't like it on my own.

Beryl Believe me, it gets better.

Ted I need you. I want you to forgive me.

Beryl Oh, is *that* all. Well, yes of course I forgive you.

Ted You do?

Beryl *Forgiving* you is easy ... it's *forgetting* that's difficult.

Ted Do you think you could?

Beryl To be honest, no.

Ted Are you prepared to try?

Beryl I don't know.

Ted You must know how you feel.

Beryl You've messed me up emotionally. I'm not sure what I feel these days.

Ted (*standing up*) You agreed to see me ... that must stand for *something*.

Beryl I agreed to see you because I thought we were going to discuss our financial arrangements.

Ted Didn't a part of you think it might be about something else?

Beryl I'd be lying if I said...

Ted What?

Beryl (*after a pause*) Well, to be honest...

Ted Say it.

Beryl You don't deserve the truth.

Ted Let me come back.

Beryl (*sitting on the arm of the* R *settee*) You haven't made a very good case for yourself.

Ted I've missed you.

Beryl That's an opportunity lost. You could have done better than that.

Ted I've had my redundancy, we could go away.

Beryl I can go away anyway.

Ted I'm lonely. I've got all this time ... all this money, but it's nothing...

Beryl (*after a pause*) Yes, go on.

Ted It's nothing ... if you haven't got anyone to share it with.

Beryl Oh, well, if it's just anyone you're looking for, you're obviously not looking hard enough.

Ted (*raising his voice*) I mean you... I want to share it with you.

Beryl There you are ... that wasn't so difficult, was it? (*She pauses*) OK ... now I *know* why you left me and I know why you want to come back. Do you think you could tell me why I should let you?

Ted (*after a pause*) No, I can't. I can't think of one reason unless it's because you still love me.

Beryl Why should I love someone that doesn't love me back?

Ted But I do. I always have. The trouble is, it got mixed up with a lot of other things. It took a long time, I know, but I've sorted myself out now. I don't want to grow old on my own. I want us to grow old together.

Beryl I'm amazed you want to grow old at all.

Ted Well, I don't ... but I've come to realize there's nothing I can do about it.

Beryl So why do you wear that ridiculous thing on your head.

Ted I admit I bought it for me at the time ... but I wore it for you tonight.

Beryl You don't have to do those sort of things for me, Ted. If you don't know that by now you'll never know it.

Ted I wanted to give it my best shot. I wanted to look good. (*He pauses*) Seems to me you wanted to as well. I've never seen you so lovely.

Beryl You think I wanted to look like this for you? (*She pauses as she moves* DR *slightly*) Six months ago perhaps ... but I dress for me now, Ted, and anyone else who cares to look.

Ted I suppose I asked for that.

Beryl (*turning to him*) If you got all you asked for...

There is a pause

Ted Look, I don't expect you to give me an answer tonight.

Beryl That's kind of you. I'm surprised you didn't say, "I'm moving in Friday, be here to give me a hand".

Ted I can, if you like.

Beryl Don't even think about it!

Ted But will *you*? Will you think about taking me back?

Beryl (*after a pause*) Yes.
Ted So you do still love me?
Beryl I don't think I ever stopped.
Ted (*after a pause*) When can I have my answer?
Beryl In a couple of days ... a week perhaps.
Ted I'll ring you the day after tomorrow.
Beryl Don't push it.
Ted No.
Beryl Things are different now.
Ted Of course.
Beryl Whatever I decide, one thing is for certain ... either way, nothing is
  going to be like it was.
Ted Completely different. A new leaf.
Beryl For both of us...
Ted I'll drink to that.
Beryl But you don't have a drink.
Ted No, I don't, do I? (*He looks at his empty glass*)
Beryl Shall I get you one?
Ted Please.

*Beryl takes his empty glass as she walks around him and makes for the curtain
pull. She opens the curtains with a swish*

Beryl What about you, Dawn?

  Dawn is standing just outside, listening

  Are you going to join us?

Music plays as the Lights fade

SCENE 5

The following week. Late afternoon

*Music fades and the Lights come up. A suitcase is now alongside the
armchair*

*Scott is standing just outside the open french windows, looking down into the
garden. He is drinking a lager straight from the bottle*

*A moment later, Angie comes in from the kitchen, carrying a tray with glasses
of cold drinks. She sets it down on the coffee table*

Angie Give Mum a shout, will you?

Scott looks at her for a second. He doesn't do as he is asked; he steps into the room

Scott Listen ... we're still friends, aren't we?
Angie (*slightly cool*) Yeah, course we are.
Scott But we're not what we were, right?
Angie I know I'm a bit cool, but I'll come round in a minute. I can't help it, rejection does this to me.
Scott It's not that I don't like you.
Angie We're a pair of no hopers however you wrap it up.
Scott It's a difficult time for me right now.
Angie Which is why you're running away.
Scott I'm not running anywhere.
Angie Sorry, I thought that was your suitcase there.
Scott Going to France was something I planned on a couple of weeks ago... (*He moves down stage, around the back of the* L *settee*) It doesn't have anything to do with putting distance between us.
Angie Perhaps a week alone will do you good anyway... I often used to go away by myself.
Scott Um... I won't be alone.
Angie What?
Scott I'm taking someone with me.

She looks at him and tries to smile. She eventually turns and moves just outside the french windows

Angie (*calling down the garden to Beryl*) Mum? Come inside and have something cold to drink. (*She steps back inside the room*)

There is an awkward pause

Scott I'm sorry.
Angie For what? There was never anything going on between us.
Scott No.
Angie (*moving to sit on the* R *settee*) So you don't have anything to apologise for, right?
Scott If things were different——
Angie Then they wouldn't be the same. Wait a minute ... you and me hasn't got anything to do with you and my mother, has it?
Scott Nothing whatsoever. (*He smiles*) Did you think it's her I'm going away with?
Angie I don't know who it is. (*She waits for him to say, but he doesn't*)

Scott Your mother is a very special lady ... and I'm going to miss her.
Angie You'll only be gone a week.
Scott But I won't be coming back ... well, not here.
Angie You won't? What did my mother say?
Scott She said there's a room here for me whether your father moves back
   in or not.
Angie Well then?
Scott (*moving to the drinks cabinet*) My moving out has got nothing to do
   with the possibility of him moving in. It's time to move on ... simple as
   that.
Angie But she needs you.
Scott No, she doesn't.
Angie All right, *I* need you.
Scott (*turning*) Then I do have something to apologise for.
Angie No, you don't... (*She moves to stand in front of the* L *settee*) I'm the
   one who's making a fool of myself.
Scott Only in front of me, and I don't count.
Angie It's not fair...
Scott I'm not the first ... and I won't be the last.
Angie What do you mean?
Scott A little birdie told me you're never short of a fella or two.
Angie It's all lies.
Scott Well, *I* believe it.
Angie (*smiling*) I know when I'm being let down gently.
Scott (*after a pause*) Are you all right?
Angie Can I ask you a favour?

He nods

   Will you kiss me?

He smiles

   I don't mean a peck on the cheek. I mean a real snog. (*She pauses*)
   Will you?

*After a pause, he walks over to her, holds her by the top of her arms and
kisses her*

   Beryl comes in wearing gardening gloves

Beryl It's unbearably hot for this time of... (*She stops briefly as she sees them
   locked together. She spots the cold drink on the coffee table and begins to
   drink it*)

Eventually Angie and Scott part

Angie (*almost without breath*) Thank you.

They both realize Beryl is in the room

Scott Oh...
Angie Mum ... you've got your orange then.
Beryl Yes... I wasn't sure whether to drink it or throw it over the pair of you.
Scott I was just doing Angie a favour.
Angie We were saying goodbye, that's all.
Beryl Angie, there's goodbye and there's good God! I don't know what it felt like to *you*, but I know what it looked like to *me*.
Scott We were just knocking it on the head.
Beryl Sealed with a loving kiss, eh?
Angie Well, you're fifty per cent right.
Scott (*after a pause*) Listen, time's getting on and I still have to pack a couple of things. (*To Angie*) Will you be here when I come back down?
Angie Probably not.
Scott Right ... well, I'll see you around then ... maybe.
Angie (*smiling*) Yeah ... maybe.

Scott leaves for upstairs

There is a pause

So ... he's moving out.
Beryl All good things...
Angie You'll miss him.
Beryl Almost as much as you.
Angie What are you going to do? You'll be on your own ... unless you take Dad back.
Beryl Being on your own isn't so bad.
Angie You're *not* taking him back, then?
Beryl I didn't say that. The situation is still under review.
Angie It's not fair to keep him hanging on.
Beryl Don't talk to me about being fair... Anyway, I've still got a day or two.

Suddenly, Dawn appears at the french windows. She is struggling to carry a suitcase

Dawn It's only me. Can I leave this in here for a minute? The last thing I want is for Dennis to catch sight of it.

Beryl goes to her and helps her bring it indoors

Angie What's going on?

Beryl You've decided to do it, then?

Dawn I didn't have the guts to tell him to his face, so I'm going to leave him a note.

Angie Are you off somewhere?

Beryl She's leaving Dennis.

Angie What?

Dawn But only for a week. I don't know what else to do. The idea is to let him fend for himself... He won't, of course, so he'll starve for seven days. If that's the only way I can get him to lose weight, then so be it.

Angie What's stopping him ringing for an Indian, or a Chinese?

Dawn Oh, he can't do that.

Angie Why not?

Dawn I've ripped the phones.

Beryl Where will you go?

Angie (*a thought suddenly hits her*) Not France by any chance?

Dawn I shouldn't think so. Why?

Angie Nothing... For one horrible minute I thought ... nothing.

Beryl You don't have to go away at all, you know. There's nothing stopping you staying here with me, providing you can cope with being stuck in the house for an entire week.

Angie And being on your own isn't so bad, you said?

Beryl I'm not suggesting it for me. I was just thinking of saving Dawn some money.

Dawn And it would ... but I've got my heart set on flying off somewhere.

Angie So you'll just buy a ticket at the airport.

Dawn That's right.

Angie That's the way to do it. I've half a mind to come with you.

Dawn Let's all three of us go.

Beryl No ... you can count me out this time. Nothing stopping *you* though, Angie.

Angie I wasn't serious.

Dawn Well, think about it. You've got until I come back in.

There is a knock at the front door

I'm just going to write Dennis that little note.

Beryl And stick it on the fridge?

Dawn Are you kidding? He'd never find it. I'm going to have to pin it to the arm of the settee.

Dawn goes out through the french windows

Beryl Are you going to go?
Angie It's a nice thought, but...
Beryl You'll be company for each other.

There is a knock on the front door

Angie I'll get it.

Angie goes off

Beryl picks up the tray and glasses and takes them out to the kitchen

A moment later, Angie comes back into the room, followed by Ted, who is not wearing his toupee

She was here a minute ago. (*She calls*) Mum?
Beryl (*off*) Yes?
Angie It's for you.

A pause before Beryl comes in from the kitchen. She sees Ted and stops in her tracks

Beryl Oh.
Ted I hadn't heard anything... I was just passing. I thought I'd pop in. (*He sees Dawn's case*) Perhaps now isn't a good time.
Beryl No, now is fine.

An awkward pause

Angie I'm er... I'm just going out the garden.

Angie goes out

Another awkward pause

Ted You going away? (*He indicates the suitcase*)
Beryl Er no... They're not mine, ours, mine. Sit down.

He sits down on the R settee

A pause

Ted It's been four days. Have you had time to think about it?

Beryl (*after a pause*) Ted, I didn't ask for what happened to me. To be honest,
I wouldn't wish it on my worst enemy… When I lost you, I thought my
world had come to an end… It hadn't of course, it had only just started. (*She
pauses*) For the first time in a long time, I began to discover *me*. I even
started to like me. (*She pauses*) I had no idea how much I liked being free
until you invited me back into the cage. (*She pauses*) I'm sorry, Ted, I'm
going to have to turn you down.

Ted I wasn't in my right mind when I left. Don't I deserve a second chance?

Beryl Of course you do … everyone does … it's just that I can't afford to
give you one. We can't go back, Ted. What you'd be asking me to give up
is too precious.

Ted It's all to do with him, isn't it? That young man that's living here.

Beryl Oh, Ted… (*She pauses*) There's nothing going on between me and
Scott any more than there was between you and that woman from accounts.
We're just good friends … and anyway, he's moving out. His girlfriend did
what you did.

Ted What's that?

Beryl She asked to come back. The only difference is, *he* said "Yes".

Ted (*after a pause*) So that's it then … it's all over.

She smiles sadly and nods

Can I see you from time to time?

Beryl I don't think that would be a good idea.

Ted How will I cope?

Beryl Oh, you'll cope… The way I see it you won't be on your own for long,
anyway. As for us … you're just going to have to bite the bullet on it.

There is a long pause between them

Ted turns and leaves

Beryl slowly sits down

*After a moment, Angie quietly comes in through the french windows. She
steps inside the room*

I suppose you heard it all?

Angie Are you all right?

Beryl I feel like… (*Very excitedly*) Dancing on the lawn.

Angie (*leaning over the arm of the settee towards Beryl*) You're sure you've
made the right decision?

Beryl No question.

Angie I'm very proud of you.

Scott returns from upstairs. He's carrying a holdall

Scott (*seeing Angie*) I thought you said you wouldn't be here.
Angie (*pretending to be put out*) Oh, I beg your pardon.
Scott (*picking up his suitcase*) I'm just going to put the bags in the car.

Scott goes out, carrying the bags

A pause

Angie And what are you going to do?
Beryl Me? I'm going to sit here when you've all gone and listen to the sound of silence ... or maybe just the birds.

Dawn comes back on through the french windows

Dawn Right that's it, I've done it.
Beryl No turning back now, then.
Dawn I've left a sink full of dishes, the bin overflowing, even the Hoover bag is full to the brim. (*To Angie*) What about you? Have you made up your mind? Are you coming?
Beryl Yes, of course she is.
Angie (*scornfully*) Mum!
Beryl If you don't, you'll only be over here every five minutes worrying about me, and I want some peace and quiet for a change.
Dawn That's settled then.
Angie I'll have to pack.
Dawn Obviously. You've got your car here?

Angie nods

Good. I'll come with you now and then we can go straight on to the airport. (*She reaches for her suitcase*)
Angie (*laughing*) I don't believe this.
Beryl You go and enjoy yourself.
Angie (*after a pause*) Right ... well, I'll go and enjoy myself then.

They hug

You're sure you'll be all right?
Beryl Don't worry about me.

Angie See you when I get back, then.
Beryl Ring and let me know where you're going.
Angie (*taking the suitcase from Dawn*) Here, let me take that.

Angie goes out

Dawn (*to Beryl*) Don't forget, *should* you see Dennis in the garden, you don't
know where I am. And if he says he doesn't know how to light the cooker,
don't you offer to do it for him.
Beryl As if.
Dawn See you in a week, then.
Beryl Yes ... enjoy...

They hug

And look after yourself.

Dawn breaks away and goes out towards the front door

*A pause. Beryl smiles and sighs heavily before going over to the drinks
cabinet and pouring herself a small sherry*

*Scott comes back into the room. He creeps up on her and frightens her
playfully*

Scott Caught red-handed!
Beryl (*giving some sort of scream*) It's only a small one, and anyway, I
reckon I deserve it.
Scott I reckon you do. (*He pauses*) I'm off now.
Beryl (*moving away* UL) Right.
Scott There's still a few things upstairs. I can pick them up when I get back
... some time next week.
Beryl Fine.
Scott (*after a pause*) Thanks ... for everything.
Beryl No ... thank *you*.

There is a pause

Scott Are you OK?

She smiles and nods

You're not going to take Ted back, are you?

Beryl How did you know?

Scott You look like the cat that got the cream.

Beryl Really? I feel as though I've got the whole damn tub.

Scott You're going to be fine.

Beryl Oh, I know I am.

Scott (*moving downstage*) I'm sure you've made the right decision.

Beryl And you?

Scott (*after a pause*) Everyone deserves a second chance.

Beryl Yes ... and you're young enough to give her one.

Scott Pardon?

Beryl A second chance.

Scott (*smiling*) Oh ... right.

Beryl (*moving downstage*) She's a very lucky girl... If I was thirty years
    younger——

Scott I wouldn't be born.

They both laugh

You do have an eye for me, then?

Beryl (*crossing* R *to him*) I don't want to own what I see. You've just given
    me the confidence to appreciate the view ... and I would like to see it from
    time to time.

Scott What you're saying is, "Don't be a stranger".

Beryl Yes.

Scott I wasn't going to be ... unless it was a problem.

Beryl For Heather?

Scott For you.

Beryl I've only got one problem.

Scott What's that?

Beryl Who's going to prune my corylopsis?

Scott You haven't got a corylopsis.

Beryl Then I'd better get one.

Scott Am I going to have to have a reason for coming here?

Beryl No, of course not. I'm really going to miss you.

Scott I'm not going to be a million miles away.

Beryl No, you're not, are you?

There is a pause. Beryl moves away DL *positioning herself in front of the* L
settee

Can I ask you a favour?

He nods

Will you kiss me?
Scott Why?
Beryl (*after a pause*) I want to feel like a woman.

After a pause, he slowly goes to her. He holds her by the top of her arms

   As he is about to kiss her, Dawn rushes on from the hallway

Dawn Angie said she can't...

Scott releases Beryl and turns to Dawn

   Angie can't get out of the drive until you move your car.
Scott Right, I'm on my way. (*He turns back to Beryl*)

She looks at him as if to say, "Oh, well ... never mind". He holds her by her arms again and kisses her in front of Dawn. Dawn can't believe her eyes. She waits and watches until they break apart

Beryl (*quietly*) Thanks.

   He turns, collects his things, and leaves, passing Dawn on his way out

Dawn watches him go

   Dawn?

Dawn turns to look at Beryl. Her jaw is almost touching the floor. Beryl taps the bottom of her own chin in an attempt at telling Dawn to close hers. Dawn obeys instinctively but the jaw drops down again immediately

   Dawn turns and goes out, leaving Beryl alone in the room

After a moment, the front door is heard closing. Beryl smiles and sighs. She slowly walks around the room before sitting. The birds are heard singing outside for a brief moment. Beryl sits alone, comfortable and happy as—

                    —the CURTAIN *falls*

FURNITURE AND PROPERTY LIST

Further dressing may be added at the director's discretion

ACT I

SCENE 1

On stage: Two settees with scatter cushions. *On one:* **Beryl**'s coat
Low coffee table. *On it:* keys, wallet, etc.
Drinks cabinet containing drinks and glasses
Bureau
Chair
Dining chair
Table lamps on occasional tables
Curtains (practical)
Magazines

Off stage: Small make-up bag containing lipstick etc. (**Dawn**)
Coat (**Ted**)

Personal: **Beryl:** watch

SCENE 2

Re-set: **Beryl**'s coat neatly over back of chair

Personal: **Ted:** watch

SCENE 3

On stage: Empty bottle

Off stage: Tray with three mugs (**Dawn**)
Club biscuit (**Dawn**)

SCENE 4

Off stage: Tray with mug of hot water, spoon, jar of Nescafé (**Dawn**)

SCENE 5

Off stage: Case, rucksack, duty-free bag (**Angie**)
               Mail (**Angie**)
               Two mugs of tea (**Scott**)

ACT II

SCENE 1

On stage: Painting tools and pots
               Cups
               Dust sheet
               Bag containing flask and sandwiches

Personal: **Dawn:** scissors

SCENE 2

Off stage: Two cans of Coke (**Angie**)
               Shopping bags, one containing dress (**Beryl**)
               Two cups of tea (**Scott**)

Personal: **Beryl:** sun hat

SCENE 3

Personal: **Angie:** watch
               Scott: small towel
               Ted: toupee

SCENE 4

On stage: Bag containing hand weights
               Two sets of dumb-bells

Scene 5

On stage: Suitcase

Off stage: Tray with glasses of cold drinks (**Angie**)
Suitcase (**Dawn**)
Holdall (**Scott**)

LIGHTING PLOT

Practical fittings required: table lamps
1 interior. The same throughout

ACT I, SCENE 1

To open: Early evening lighting

Cue 1   **Beryl** breaks down   (Page 6)
             Fade to black-out

ACT I, SCENE 2

To open: Table lamp lit

Cue 2   **Ted** switches on the lights   (Page 7)
             Fade up general lighting

Cue 3   **Beryl** breaks down   (Page 12)
             Fade to black-out

ACT I, SCENE 3

To open: Minimal light from small table lamp, chink of daylight through
             curtains

Cue 4   **Angie** opens the curtains   (Page 13)
             Daylight

Cue 5   **Beryl** ponders   (Page 20)
             Fade to black-out

ACT I, SCENE 4

To open: Mid-afternoon lighting

Cue 6   All fall about laughing   (Page 27)
             Black-out

ACT I, SCENE 5

To open: Dark, with daylight outside

Cue 7   **Angie** opens the curtains   (Page 28)
             Daylight

Cue 8   Music plays   (Page 38)
             Fade to black-out

ACT II, SCENE 1

To open: Mid-morning lighting

Cue 9   Music plays   (Page 45)
             Fade to black-out

ACT II, SCENE 2

To open: Late afternoon lighting

Cue 10   Music plays   (Page 54)
             Fade to black-out

ACT II, SCENE 3

To open: Interior lighting, practicals on. Evening exterior lighting

Cue 11   Music plays   (Page 62)
             Fade to black-out

ACT II, SCENE 4

To open: Interior lighting, practicals on

Cue 12   Music plays   (Page 74)
             Fade to black-out

ACT II, SCENE 5

To open: Late afternoon lighting

*No cue*s

EFFECTS PLOT

ACT I

Cue 1   **Beryl**: "Will you say it like you mean it?"   (Page 6)
After a pause, taxi horn sounds off

Cue 2   **Beryl** breaks down   (Page 6)
Music; fade when ready

Cue 3   **Beryl** breaks down   (Page 12)
Music; fade when ready

Cue 4   **Beryl** is slumped on the L settee   (Page 12)
Front door slams

Cue 5   **Angie** leaves   (Page 19)
Front door closes

Cue 6   **Beryl** is left to ponder   (Page 20)
Music; fade when ready

Cue 7   **Angie**: "I hope so."   (Page 23)
Doorbell rings

Cue 8   Black-out   (Page 27)
Music; fade when ready

Cue 9   Voices are heard off   (Page 27)
Front door slams

Cue 10   **Angie**: "I mean, look at me."   (Page 30)
Lawnmower starts up

Cue 11   **Beryl** opens french windows   (Page 31)
Increase lawnmower noise

Cue 12   **Beryl** waits hesitantly   (Page 31)
Lawnmower stops

| *Cue* 13 | **Angie** and **Dawn** are stunned into silence | (Page 38) |
| | *Music; to end* | |

ACT II

| *Cue* 14 | To open | (Page 39) |
| | *Music; cross-fade to radio music when ready* | |

| *Cue* 15 | **Scott** turns the radio off | (Page 40) |
| | *Cut music* | |

| *Cue* 16 | **Dawn** begins to cut **Beryl**'s hair | (Page 45) |
| | *Music; fade when ready* | |

| *Cue* 17 | **Scott** and **Angie** almost kiss | (Page 48) |
| | *Front door slams* | |

| *Cue* 18 | **Beryl** rams her hat into a shopping bag | (Page 54) |
| | *Music; fade when ready* | |

| *Cue* 19 | **Angie**: "…wait till she gets back." | (Page 56) |
| | *Kitchen door slams* | |

| *Cue* 20 | **Beryl**: "That'll confuse things at the Post Office." | (Page 61) |
| | *Knock on front door* | |

| *Cue* 21 | **Beryl** and **Ted** look at each other | (Page 62) |
| | *Music; fade when ready* | |

| *Cue* 22 | **Angie**: "Are you, Mum … happy?" | (Page 67) |
| | *After a pause, knock on front door* | |

| *Cue* 23 | **Beryl**: "Are you going to join us?" | (Page 74) |
| | *Music; fade when ready* | |

| *Cue* 24 | **Dawn**: "You've got until I come back in." | (Page 78) |
| | *Knock on front door* | |

| *Cue* 25 | **Beryl**: "You'll be company for each other." | (Page 79) |
| | *Knock on front door* | |

| *Cue* 26 | **Dawn** goes out | (Page 84) |
| | *After a moment, front door closes* | |

| *Cue* 27 | **Beryl** sits down | (Page 84) |
| | *Birds singing outside for a brief moment* | |